SAUVIE ISLAND
A Step Back in Time
Second Edition

KiKi Canniff

ISBN: 978-0941361-491

Copyright © 1981, 2014 by KiKi Canniff

No part of this book may be reproduced in any form, including but not limited to printed, electronic and mechanical means, information storage and retrieval systems, without permission in writing from the publisher.

Cover Design

Heather Kibbey - Northwest Publishers Consortium, Lake Oswego, OR
www.NPCBooks.com

Photographs & Illustrations

Photo credits: Most of the historic photos used in the first edition of this book also appear in this updated edition. Many new photographs have been added as well.

The Indian bones photograph in Chapter 3 and aerial flood photograph in Chapter 7 appear courtesy of the Oregon Historical Society; all other flood photographs in Chapter 7 were taken by E. Vetsch. All of these photographs are from the original edition. All other photographs contained in this book were taken by the author.

Illustration credits: The pen and Ink illustrations are by Cathy Dvorak, and are also from the first edition.

Sauvie Island; A Step Back in Time

TABLE OF CONTENTS

Introduction 5

Chapter One
    Sauvie Island, Oregon - One Island with
        Many Names 9

Chapter Two
    Oregon History - As Witnessed by Sauvie Island 15

Chapter Three
    Wakanasese Island - The Indians' Island 19

Chapter Four
    Multnomah Island - The Land of Explorers and
        Fur Traders 31

Chapter Five
    Wyeth Island - An East Coast Entrepreneur
        Builds a Town 39

Chapter Six
    Sauvie Island - Oregon Territory Established
        and Island Settled 49

Chapter Seven
    How the Rising Water Affected Island Life 65

Chapter Eight
    Time Brings Changes and a Bridge to the Mainland .. 79

Chapter Nine
    The Sauvie Island Wildlife Management Area 89

Chapter Ten
    Exploring Sauvie Island in the Twenty-First Century . 93
        Getting the Most from Your Island Visit 93

Exploring the Island 95
Gilliam Road – The Scenic Route 96
Reeder Road - The Connection 105
    Oak Island Detour 106
    Back on Reeder Road 107
Sauvie Island Road - The Channel Route 107
    From the Bridge to Reeder Road 108
    All the Way to the End 109
Touring the Island by Boat 111

Appendix
    Sauvie Island Plants, Trees & Wildlife 115
Index 123

INTRODUCTION

This book was originally published in 1981; that first print run was small and copies have been unavailable for decades. Sauvie Island has changed very little since then; other than the new bridge installed in 2009 it has remained relatively unspoiled.

When this book was first written, I lived on the island and had the time to hike and canoe every bit of its public land. I seldom encountered others back then, except during the summer and on weekends. Things are a little busier now as more mainland residents discover the island's nearby serenity and historic beauty.

Sauvie Island's first non-native visitors had to come by sailing ship around the Cape, or by wagon train across the Oregon Trail; the journey took months. Today it takes less than 30 minutes to reach Sauvie Island from downtown Portland.

And, although urban sprawl creeps through the hills from all directions, and the old Indian trails now transport workers to jobs in neighboring valleys, the island remains a quiet retreat.

In the back of this book you'll learn all about the island's recreational opportunities, but first I'd like to share the tale of Sauvie Island's history as recorded by explorers, 19th century entrepreneurs, early visitors and pioneer families.

The original research for this book was done in a very hands-on manner. I spent many happy days up to my elbows in research, excitedly digging for island history in the archives of the Oregon Historical Society Library.

I read all of the journals and diaries written by early explorers, examined Sauvie Island and Portland family scrapbooks, and looked through boxes of pioneer treasures.

Back on the island, I interviewed descendants of the original pioneer families, and was privileged to see private collections of island memorabilia. These generous individuals also shared their oral history; retelling to me the family stories they had heard as children. It is their story that I share with you.

Most of the material in this book appeared in the first edition. The final chapters were updated to provide current details on island parks, historic areas, hiking trails, boating spots, u-pick farms, annual events and public access.

The map on the following page shows how to get to Sauvie Island from Portland or St. Helens.

Sauvie Island; A Step Back in Time

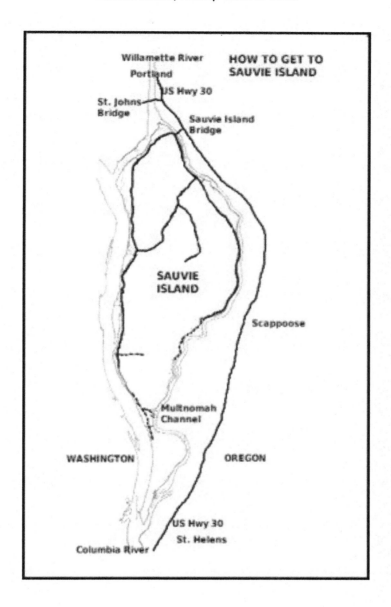

CHAPTER ONE

Sauvie Island, Oregon
One Island with Many Names

Twelve miles northwest of downtown Portland you'll find a 24,000 acre island with few houses, lots of natural beauty, and fertile flatlands. Relatively unpopulated, it is sprinkled with lakes and lapped by water on all sides.

Three snow-capped mountains can be seen from the island, Mount St. Helens, Mt. Adams and Mt. Hood. On a sunny day these mountains add a gorgeous backdrop to Sauvie Island's pastoral setting.

Sauvie Island; A Step Back in Time

Located on what some believe to be the prettiest river highway in America, Sauvie Island (pronounced Saw-vee) played an important role in early Oregon history.

Its fields and beaches have held the camps of Indians, explorers, opportunists, scientists and pioneers. The Willamette Valley's first city was built on this island more than a decade before Portland was laid out.

But, it wasn't until 1950 that Sauvie Island became permanently linked to the mainland. Prior to that the only way to reach or leave the island had been by water. And water was sometimes the reason for leaving; twice each year the river rose up the island banks and flowed across its land.

Today that water is held back by dikes, and a bridge connects the island to U.S. Highway 30 north of Portland. On a clear day as you cross the bridge onto the island you can see one to three snow-covered mountains.

For centuries rich topsoil has been washed out of the surrounding mountains, hills and valleys by annual rains and thawing snow to land on Sauvie Island. The farmers work hard to conserve that fertile soil by using the best techniques available.

Major island crops include vegetables, berries, herbs, flowers, grains, potatoes, pumpkins and nursery stock. For over one hundred years dairy products were the island's largest industry, but not any longer. This island was named after its first dairyman.

In 1838 Laurent Sauvé, a Hudson Bay Company employee, was moved to the island to build and operate a dairy for nearby Fort Vancouver. The common practice of referring to the island as his is what led to its name.

More than half of the land is within the Sauvie Island Wildlife Management Area. Here, the Oregon Department of Fish and Wildlife works to preserve and develop the island for wintering waterfowl. Within its boundaries you'll find lots of places where you can hunt, fish, hike, picnic, boat, sunbathe, swim and run your dogs.

Historic records show the island has had many names. It was known as **Wakanasese Island** when populated by the Multnomah Indians. They were a busy and prosperous tribe, trading wapato (wop-pa-toe) root with Coastal and Mountain tribes.

Wapato Island was the name recorded in the journals belonging to the Lewis & Clark Expedition. These men camped on the island in 1805, naming it for the tuberous wapato that grew in abundance in island marshes and lake beds.

In 1834 Boston businessman Nathaniel J. Wyeth established the location of this region's first city, which he built on Sauvie Island.

Wyeth believed his city would someday become the head of shipping for the entire area. Bad luck, accidents, ill health and discouragement led to Wyeth's departure in 1836. After that, both the British and Americans referred to it as **Wyeth Island**.

When the United States Exploring Expedition commanded by Commodore Charles Wilkes visited in 1841 the island was again renamed.

Wilkes called it **Multnomah Island**, for the tribes that had once populated its land. This is the name recorded on a map dated 1855 and published by J.H. Colton & Company.

There are nine spellings of the island's current name with the two most popular being S-A-U-V-I-E and S-A-U-V-I-E-S. The first is listed by the U.S. Board of Geographic Names as correct; the second is the way islanders have spelled it for generations. This is the spelling used on all of the old county road signs, the old school, ferries, church, maps and island organizations.

New faces brought new ways, and sometimes you'll see signs that have the singular spelling right alongside older signs with the "s" on the end.

Other spellings of that same name have included:

S-A-U-V-E

S-A-U-V-I-E-'S

S-A-H-V-E-E

S-O-V-E-E-S

S-O-V-A-Y

S-A-W-V-A-Y-S

S-O-P-H-I-E-S

Add those nine different spellings to Wakanasese, Wapato, Wyeth and Multnomah Island, and it could get pretty confusing as to exactly where you happened to be.

There are now three primary roads on the island; together they form a loop of about twelve miles beginning and ending at the bridge. These flat roads make bicycling fun when the traffic is light.

Paved roads also allow access to the Sauvie Island Wildlife Management Area. These lead to a network of flat gravel and dirt roadways, and short trails that provide easy country hiking.

Every fall migrating swans, ducks and geese visit the island in huge numbers. Spring again brings the waterfowl through, along with their young, on their return trip north. This makes it a terrific place for bird watching.

Many exceptional birds, such as the Red-tailed Hawk and Great Blue Heron, can be seen here year round. The island's abundance of lakes also provides an inviting habitat for all kinds of small mammals, ducks and shorebirds.

Fishing, swimming and boating are popular along the river banks. Inland lakes are good for fishing and offer terrific opportunities for people who like to kayak or canoe.

From early June to the end of October island farmers harvest their crops. These are sold to canneries, markets, and available as u-pick crops fresh from the farm.

Lots of local families visit those island fields late each spring when Oregon strawberries make their appearance, come back throughout the summer for fresh vegetables, and return again in the fall when the pumpkins are ripe.

The current island population is just over one thousand, and half of the island is privately owned. Some of those residents are descendants of the original pioneer families.

CHAPTER TWO

Oregon History
As Witnessed by Sauvie Island

Indians, explorers and settlers all left their mark on Sauvie Island history. There have even been claims made that two thousand years ago this island may have been home to a culture that is now both extinct and forgotten.

This claim is based on unusual stone sculptures found on the island which appear to represent an elaborate civilization that flourished far beyond simple existence. Because these stone sculptures have always been found by themselves, it has been difficult to establish exactly when the marks were first carved.

These early sculptures appear to be representative of the Fraser River Culture, a tribe that left behind stone carvings and human figures of exceptional artistry and craftsmanship. Sauvie Island sculptures fit into that category.

One island sculpture belonging to the Oregon Historical Society resembles a beaver when viewed from one direction, and an owl if looked at upside down. Other island sculptures show the faint traces of red, black and white native paint.

Most experts believe these well-crafted basalt carvings are actually the work of the Multnomah Indians, the tribe mentioned in the journals of early explorers.

The Multnomah Indians were members of the Chinook tribe; archaeological evidence documents their occupation of Sauvie Island for hundreds of years.

This is the Native American tribe that visited with the explorers and fur traders, and it is the letters and journals of those men that tell us most of what we know about their customs and traditions.

Sauvie Island was witness to many 'firsts' for this region; they are revealed throughout this book.

The island was the location for the territory's first criminal trial, held on July 4, 1835. Presided over by a minister from the Methodist mission, the entire proceedings were heard in front of a jury, making it the state's first jury trial as well.

As the story goes, Thomas J. Hubbard a gunsmith at Fort William, Wyeth's island city, had a dispute with Thornburgh, the town tailor. They argued about a native girl and Thornburgh threatened Hubbard's life. Hubbard grew fearful and slept with a loaded pistol under his pillow.

Thornburgh entered Hubbard's home early one morning armed with a loaded gun and a large knife. Awakened by his entrance, Hubbard took aim and fired his pistol. He then tossed the wounded man out into the street where he died a few minutes later.

The jury declared this to be a clear case of self-defense and came back with a verdict of justifiable homicide.

Although Nathaniel Wyeth's only stayed here for a couple of years, some of the men he brought with him to Sauvie Island remained in Oregon for their entire lives. These were the men who settled the Willamette Valley.

Wyeth brought scientists, missionaries, teachers and laborers when he came west; he also opened a wagon road crossing the Blue Mountains, a route that would soon become an important part of the Oregon Trail.

Sauvie Island also played a big part in early shipbuilding for the Oregon Territory. When the first seagoing vessel built in this region was being designed, the builders chose a tall straight fir tree from the island.

This island tree became the 48'8" timber that not only supported the entire boat frame from stem to stern, but also determined the ship's final length.

The building of this seagoing clipper ship marked the beginning of Oregon's shipbuilding industry and helped to put the American colonization of the Pacific Northwest on its feet.

When that first ship, the *Star of Oregon*, was launched in 1841 it sailed to San Francisco where it was sold, and the money was used to purchase 350 head of cattle. The following spring they returned overland with the livestock, bringing with them new settlers, many with livestock of their own, and giving a huge boost to the region's economy.

Sauvie Island; A Step Back in Time

CHAPTER THREE

Wakanasese Island; the Indians' Island

The island was a good place to live if you were a young brave in the early 1800's. Once a boy had grown past the process of having his head flattened, life was fairly simple.

Infant children sometimes died during the head flattening process since it required cording the baby down, causing the back of the head to lie flat against a small board while a second piece of wood was fixed across the forehead to slant it like the line of the nose.

When it wasn't fatal, this process was generally quite successful. Referred to as Flathead Indians by the tribesmen, their sloping heads were considered a mark of distinction.

Living along the shore, the native island children learned to respect the water early or they didn't survive. Even in play the little ones mimicked the work of their parents, and before long they were contributing to the tribes' well-being.

The Multnomah Indians lived in board houses on the island. Built entirely of cedar, and before the age of power tools, an immense amount of labor was involved in their construction.

First the trees had to be felled by burning. The men then carved giant planks from the trunks using wedges made of stone, elk horn, gnarled roots or knots.

Each board had to be about twenty feet long, two to three feet wide, and three or four inches thick. These would be used to make the sides of the house; cedar bark would adorn the roof.

A large board house would have been about one hundred feet long and forty feet wide. They were designed to shelter several families.

Each family would have had a private entrance and an individual fire pit with its own exhaust hole in the roof. The house was built over a two to three foot deep rectangular pit, which was lined with boards and covered with mats.

The island villages had a native population of about two thousand, nearly twice that of the current residents. Small villages were built in clearings, and temporary camps were scattered along the shores, providing shelter for nearby tribes who came to fish and gather wapato root on the island.

There was no need for horses here; cedar canoes carried the Indians anywhere they needed to go. Each elaborately decorated canoe was carved from the trunk of a single tree.

These boats sported elongated bows that ran four to five feet past the waterline, and they generally had symbols of bears or men painted or carved on both the bow and stern.

The larger canoes could carry twenty-five to thirty men, each with a five foot ash paddle. They must have made a spectacular sight as they silently made their way through the water.

Once a native canoe was started it was continually worked on throughout the builder's lifetime. Carving and burning decorations would have filled many an idle hour.

Island Indians were busy; they speared salmon and sturgeon from the shore or caught them with finely-woven flax nets. When they tired of fish, the hunter would head off to stalk deer near one of the island lakes.

The construction of fishing nets, stone sinkers, arrows with stone heads, and tools and implements for day-to-day living also required much work.

Indian women were kept busy gathering, cooking and cleaning. Although the wealthy island squaw had slaves there was still much to be done. Baskets had to be woven, and food picked, dug, gathered or skinned, plus food had to be prepared and dried for winter.

The principal food for the tribe was salmon or sturgeon; when fish were plentiful hunting was unnecessary. Camas and wapato roots were also important foods.

Wapato grew in great abundance on the island. To the Indians it was both potato and bread. It was also an item that gave them great wealth. Mountain and coastal tribes would trade skins, woven mats, food and other articles of value for wapato.

In 1805 the Lewis & Clark Expedition purchased four bushels of wapato root from the island Indians. At the time of this trade several members of the expedition were reported to be very ill; this addition to their diet was noted as having revived and strengthened the sick men.

The gathering of wapato was left to the women of the tribe; they used a canoe created only for this purpose. Measuring ten to fourteen feet in length, these little canoes were just eighteen to twenty-three inches at their widest point.

The boats tapered down to nothing at both ends, and were about nine inches deep. Each could carry one small person and several bushels of roots. When empty, the women could easily carry them overland to where the roots were most abundant.

Taking these miniature canoes to the edge of a pond, they would wade naked into the water pushing the boats along beside them. Loosening the roots with their toes, the tubers would float to the top and the women would put them into the canoe.

They would spend several hours in water up to their armpits; working until the boat was full. Much of this harvest was dried for future meals.

The island's native residents were known collectively as the Multnomah Indians. In reality, this group consisted of many different tribes who lived peacefully together here, fishing, hunting and gathering the wild plants.

These people were led by Chief Cassino, a noble man who was both energetic and wealthy. Cassino was an important leader; he ruled tribes for a sixty mile distance between the Cascade

Mountains and the sea, along both sides of the Columbia River.

Remembered for his intelligence and kindness, Cassino was often mentioned in the diaries of early explorers as being a friend to the white man.

Every year island natives held big celebrations and fairs. Indians from nearby mountains, rivers, valleys and the ocean would come to exchange goods, race horses and canoes, dance, and join together in celebration. They dined on elaborate feasts that were prepared by the men. It is estimated that an additional 4,000 Natives may have been present on the island during these celebrations.

The island Indians had little fear of attack and lived openly. They led a peaceful existence with simple pleasures, and when their time was up they were given a stately canoe burial.

The dead Indian was first bathed and wrapped in robes or mats before being laid out in his or her best canoe. This canoe was then propped amongst the rocks on the downstream end of the island or placed in the branches of a riverside tree.

All of the Indian's personal property, their bows and arrows, gun, salmon spears, ornaments and other prized possessions, were placed inside and around the canoe. This was done in case there was a need for such goods in future lives, but it also ended any quarrels over the possessions of the deceased.

The burial canoe was given a hole for drainage and placed in a slanted position so that the rain water could escape. This also rendered the canoe useless, making its theft undesirable. To protect the body, a second canoe was inverted over the top. Strips of bark were then carefully arranged over everything.

The natives would then set to wailing and singing songs in honor of the dead. Relatives and friends would bring presents to set beside the canoe coffin.

Thirty years after Lewis & Clark had estimated the Native population to be nearly 2,000 this sacred place was devastated by disease.

It happened so quickly that most of the bodies were left unburied, their bones lying where they had died. Grass and brush had already begun to overgrow the villages, where utensils and tools were still laid out, when this terrible devastation was discovered.

This once great seat of power was destroyed by sickness. The epidemic has been referred to as both smallpox and malaria, but whether it was brought overland by trappers and traders or from across the ocean by sailing ships, it took with it all but a few of the island's original inhabitants.

Tribes for miles around were brought nearly to extinction by the epidemic. If the illness didn't kill them the cure often did. A length of time in a sweat house, followed by a plunge into the icy river was the cure; it often brought about immediate collapse. Those who survived the disease were mostly Natives who had been denied access to the sweat lodges.

In 1830 when George Roberts, an employee of the Hudson Bay Company, came to the island to call upon Chief Cassino he found dead bodies everywhere. Legend tells us that Roberts heard a crying baby which he removed from its mother's dead grasp, and took back to Fort Vancouver.

When Roberts reported the situation to Dr. John McLoughlin, the Chief Factor for the British, the good doctor convinced ailing Chief Cassino to forego the customary sweat lodge treatment, which probably saved his life.

Chief Cassino survived to rule an empty nation. His own house was reduced from ten wives, four children and eighteen slaves to one of each. The British doctor had the survivors removed and their houses burned to the ground to stop the spreading sickness.

The island was left empty and an entire culture abandoned. When the settlers later cleared the land for farming, they found huge piles of bones and lots of artifacts.

Traces of the island's Native American residents can be found on the island even today. The remains of at least fifteen village sites have been discovered over the years. Annual flooding, along with the ever-moving river, has washed away many. Farming, and a need to build on the island's highest land, obliterated the rest.

Archeological Investigations Northwest, a group staffed by students from South Puget Sound Community College, have mapped and documented the old Sunken Village Site on the downriver end of the island.

Items found at this 350-yard-long beachside village suggest that this part of the island has been the location of Indian gatherings for at least 3,000 years. The dig site is not open to the public.

The Sunken Village Dig has been designated as a National Historic Landmark by the National Park Service. They found more than 60 acorn pits at this site, the largest number ever uncovered, making this a site of significant importance.

Each acorn pit consisted of a hand-dug hole that had been lined with hemlock boughs and filled with about 1,000 acorns. These were dug where underground springs empty into the channel allowing the spring water to rush through the pits; over the course of one winter the water would remove toxins, making the acorns edible by spring.

Simple cattail mat structures, wood and plant fibers, stone blades, cedar-bark matting, root cordage, tool making remains, and an intact checker-weave cedar basket were also found.

These digs were overseen by Confederated Tribe members, and all items found are eventually destined for display at Oregon tribal museums. Until then, they are stored at the University of Oregon.

Early visitors found Native American bodies lying openly on the ground when they arrived and piles of Indian artifacts in the old village refuse heaps.

When pioneer farmers tilled the soil they often unearthed artifacts. Huge caches of fishing sinkers, like those shown below with the mortar and pestle were discovered beneath the soil's surface.

Grinding stones, arrowheads, game stones, beads, copper bracelets, paint pots and trade buttons were among the artifacts found on the island. The high quality of the ornaments, bowls, baskets, carved bone and stone images, banded and perforated sinkers attest to the great skills of this island tribe.

Hunting and foraging for food took the Indians all over the island. Even now, a heavy spring frost will sometimes pop arrowheads to the surface along the lake shores; heavy rain does the same thing.

Petroglyphs and native rock drawings were impossible to create where the land was so flat, so the island occupants created carved images.

One well-carved four-cornered column mentioned in the journals of early traders was reportedly used by the Natives as a rain fetish and thought to be inhabited by spirits. The Indians were said to believe that when touched, this carved image would bring rain. The wet Oregon climate must have kept this spirit very busy.

Island settlers referred to this column as the Multnomah Stone. A heavy block of basalt, it was four to five feet high and about three feet in diameter. When the farmer on whose land it rested cleared the land for tilling, it was rolled over the bank and into the channel.

Other carved images were found on the island as well. Many are housed in private collections while others were given to the Oregon Historical Society.

A two-hundred-pound stone owl and a smaller frog, or toad-like creature, are among those in public collections. The carvings' lines and images are still very clear and distinct.

These stone carvings are representative of the sculptures that some believe were left behind by an earlier culture. However, until one of them is found buried along with other artifacts we will continue to wonder about their true origin.

Sauvie Island; A Step Back in Time

CHAPTER FOUR

Multnomah Island
The Land of Explorers and Fur Traders

In May of 1792, just two years after becoming the first American to circumnavigate the globe, Captain Robert Gray entered the Columbia River. He named this river for his ship.

Sailing for a group of east coast businessmen, Captain Gray's crew had traded goods all up and down the coast. They had filled their ship with furs exchanged for blankets, beads, brass buttons, earrings, calico cloth, tin mirrors, hunting knives, copper nails, copper kettles, iron chisels, snuff and tobacco.

It was during his second visit to the Columbia River that Gray made his discovery of the river entrance. He immediately held a short ceremony, claiming all land drained by the Columbia for America, before heading upstream.

He and his crew were the first white men to enter the river that day when he took his eighty-three foot ship, which sported three masts, across the treacherous Columbia River Bar.

Gray's expert navigation was responsible for this impressive feat; he took his boat closer to shore than any other captain before him had dared. For more than two centuries entrance to this river had remained elusive to passing ships.

When British Captain George Vancouver learned of this accomplishment he quickly rushed to top it. Less than six months after Gray, he too entered the river. Vancouver and his men intended to outdo the Americans by exceeding their thirty-six mile exploration.

Vancouver sent Lt. William Broughton up the Columbia to survey it for the British Admiralty. Broughton and his men crossed the bar aboard the 138-ton brig *H.M.S. Chatham*. From there they preceded upriver much further than Gray by using the ship's two smaller boats.

As they travelled the explorers made journal entries, drew maps recording natural landmarks, and named mountains, islands and land points. These were the men who first charted the Columbia River.

Broughton's first glimpse with Sauvie Island was when he and his men were approached by twenty-three Indian canoes near the island's north end.

The canoes held 150 or more Natives dressed in war garments. After speaking with the explorers the friendly island natives removed their war garments and weapons.

Broughton named that northern point Warrior Rock in honor of the peaceful natives who had come dressed for war and ended up staying to trade. According to journal entries, only the visitors' copper swords and iron battle axes escaped the exchange.

Mistaking the Multnomah Channel for a river, Broughton named it Calls River after a British military engineer. He then continued east on the Columbia River, scouting the Sauvie Island shore.

That evening Broughton and his men became the first white men to ever land on the island when they took shelter beneath a row of willows along the Columbia River.

The next day they discovered the entrance to the Willamette River, noting that two small islands were also located there. Broughton named that Sauvie Island point Belle Vue Point. Dredging has closed the old channel, and those smaller islands are now part of the big island at Willow Bar Slough.

It was from Belle Vue Point that the British commander first spotted what he described in his log book as a *"very distant high, snowy mountain rising beautifully conspicuous in the midst of an extensive tract of low or moderately elevated land."*

Awed by the sight of this majestic mountain, as seen from Sauvie Island, he named it Mt. Hood in honor of a famous countryman. The view is just as impressive today.

Early in November the Lieutenant and his men passed by the island once more on their return to the ship. After that, the island and its inhabitants were left alone until 1805, when it was once again visited by explorers. This time they were Americans.

In 1803 President Thomas Jefferson appointed Meriwether Lewis to find a passage west. Lewis wisely chose William Clark as his co-commander and it became known as the Lewis and Clark Expedition.

The two men met at the Ohio River in Illinois, where they purchased equipment and supplies and recruited volunteers. On May 14, 1804 a group of forty-five men left to begin the expedition by heading up the Missouri River.

It took them until October of 1805 to reach the Columbia River; they had come over the Rocky Mountains in search of a river that would lead to the Pacific Ocean. The expedition headed downriver in thirty wooden canoes.

During their journey they passed right by the mouth of the Willamette River, assuming that Sauvie Island was the mainland. Stopping for lunch on the island, Clark's journal entries state that he walked three miles along the shore.

That night the men camped near a small sand island, according to journal entries, which puts them on the same beach where Lt. Broughton and his men had stayed seven years earlier.

The Lewis and Clark Expedition explorers kept detailed journals as they travelled, and notes made about that first night on Sauvie Island were not at all favorable.

They complained that *"huge flocks of geese, swans, ducks and other birds serenaded them with a confusion of noises preventing them from sleeping."* They had arrived during fall migration.

Those journals also tell us the bulk of what we know about the Multnomah Indians. Lewis and Clark were the first to apply this name to the tribe that lived on the island.

They raved about the Indians' canoes, calling them the finest in the world, both as to their use and beauty. The Indians themselves were described as experts in handling watercraft.

It was William Clark who wrote about the naked Indian women and their wapato harvesting canoes, describing how they loosened the root of the plant from its bed beneath the water. The explorers' time on the island was not spent idly.

After completing their journey to the sea, Lewis and Clark passed the island once more on their return trip. In the spring of 1806 they made camp on the Washington shore, directly opposite their previous Sauvie Island encampment.

Recalling that sleepless night in November they had positioned themselves where they could enjoy this beautiful but noisy island from a distance. The seemingly endless flocks of birds were still visible from their camp.

The following morning they paddled across the river and ate breakfast near their old campsite. Once again they wrote that their ears rang with the sounds of noisy waterfowl. Those journals mention many of the noisemakers by name.

They saw several Indian fishing camps along the river bank plus lots of Indians offshore in canoes. Several canoes from two of the nearby villages came to trade; the men swapped fish hooks for sturgeon and wapato, and wrote that the Indians seemed to enjoy haggling for their price.

Underway once again, the explorers left still thinking the island was part of the mainland. It was an old Washougal Indian man who set them straight, drawing a map showing this land as an island.

Equipped with a map drawn with charcoal on a tanned skin, the men found the entrance to the Willamette River. Before leaving the island this time, they sketched and labeled it in their journal, showing the location of several Indian camps.

These explorers made a fairly adequate charting of the island's existence, and their journals provide tremendous insight into life on the island.

In 1811 two more visits by explorers were recorded. The first was made by Gabriel Franchere, one of the founders of the Astoria Trading Post. His writings tell of the island's two largest Indian villages located along the beach.

The second visitor, David Thompson, was a surveyor and explorer for the British Northwest Company. He travelled up the Columbia River with seven men. On their return journey they wrote that they found the island almost entirely under water; this was in July.

Sauvie Island stands out in the letters and journals of these two 1811 explorers; it was noted as an island of considerable size, with a large but peaceful Indian population.

According to the detailed notes that Thompson kept of his travels, the high water allowed them to make their journey along the calmer channel, avoiding the strong winds raging on the Columbia.

Later, they reportedly paddled across the island itself, through Big Sturgeon Lake, arriving back on the Columbia River near Reeder Point.

As the demand for beaver pelts grew, trappers and traders came to this region in large numbers. The Hudson Bay Company, a British concern, set up their headquarters a few miles upriver from the island on the north side of the Columbia River where they built Fort Vancouver.

Dr. John McLoughlin then became the Chief Factor, and by this title, the master of Oregon Country.

Called the White Eagle by local Indians because of his shoulder-length white hair, he ruled the Pacific Northwest from the Rocky Mountains to the Pacific Ocean, California to Alaska from 1824 to 1845. Everyone respected and obeyed him, and the Multnomah Indians were no exception.

CHAPTER FIVE

Wyeth Island
An East Coast Entrepreneur Builds a Town

In 1832 a young ice merchant left Massachusetts to challenge the Hudson Bay Company's ironclad grip along the Columbia River.

Nathaniel Wyeth left everything behind, abandoning his family and a successful business in the east, to lead his expedition to the northwest in search of fur and fortune.

Wyeth's vision included a trading post, along with the first fish processing factory on the Columbia River. His plan was to send salmon, fur, produce and lumber downriver in the name of the Columbia River Fishing & Trading Company.

At the start of his journey he made an attempt to harden his east coast crew with several days of camping on an island in the Boston harbor. Some left immediately; Wyeth and the remaining twenty men headed west. He did this because he believed that only the hardiest of men could hope to complete the journey.

Wyeth added and lost men all along the way; some deserted, others were dismissed, and one man lost his life in an Indian fight at Pierre's Hole. Only eleven men made it all the way to Fort Vancouver.

Disappointing news met the men at the fort. The ship that was carrying their supplies had been wrecked in the Society

Islands; running up on an uncharted reef it had been pounded to pieces. Without goods to trade with the natives, and the tools and supplies they would need, their venture was doomed.

Wyeth's and his men had suffered every trial, danger and hardship the journey west could hand out. They had reached the fort weary and relieved, with their clothing worn out and hanging in tatters.

Five of the remaining men left on the next Hudson Bay Company ship headed for the east coast, and one man died. The men who survived that journey and stayed became some of Oregon's most revered pioneers.

Two of those men, John Ball and Calvin Tibbits, stayed on at Fort Vancouver. During the winter of 1832 John Ball taught school at the fort; this was the first school established west of the Rockies, and he was Washington's first school teacher.

Both men went on to become farmers; John Ball and Calvin Tibbits were the first Americans to farm in Oregon. After obtaining seeds and supplies from Fort Vancouver they left Wyeth's company for good.

While most of the men were leaving, Wyeth was making plans to return again. He and his crew, now down to two men, returned overland to Boston the following spring. Wyeth arrived even more enthusiastic about his plan, and ready to outfit and begin a second expedition.

On this second journey west Wyeth left Boston with seventy men. He stopped in Idaho to set up his first trading post, Fort

Hall. This fort would soon become an important stop for everyone travelling the Oregon Trail.

Wyeth was on familiar land when he crossed the mountains in 1834, and they quickly arrived at the Columbia River. At Fort Vancouver he was once again hit with bad news. The ship he had sent ahead had been struck by lightning at sea and would be delayed for repairs.

When the supplies finally came upriver on the *May Dacre*, Wyeth and his crew had Captain Lambert anchor near Sauvie Island's Warrior Rock. Although the island itself was now deserted, Indians from nearby camps up and downriver came to visit the ship every day.

Wyeth and his men quickly unloaded the goods, setting up a temporary camp on the point. They prepared a cargo of timber, loaded the ship, and sent it back to the Sandwich Islands for more supplies.

Surveying the island, Wyeth chose a permanent location for his city. He decided to locate it along the channel, opposite the overland route used by the Indians when they visited the Willamette and Tualatin Valleys.

Wyeth's men built this city on the site of the former Cath-Lah-Nal-Qui-Ah Village, two hundred feet from shore. The high ground faced the Multnomah Channel, providing a view of timber covered mountains. Behind the city a rolling prairie and open woodland could be seen, and wildlife was in abundance.

The men set to work building Fort William, and they soon had several log houses, a strong storehouse, and shops for working iron and wood.

The streets were laid out and the men moved into town. The coopers set to work building barrels for the fish; other men began the construction of a sixty-foot canoe and a larger watercraft with a cabin for their salmon business.

In late April the *May Dacre* returned once again; this time it was filled with cattle, sheep, goats, poultry and hogs. These were taken to the small barns the men had prepared.

Seeds had come too, and before long wheat, corn, potatoes, peas, beans and turnips were planted. An island orchard was started as well.

That year the weather was exceptionally bad; sickness, drowning and fighting took seventeen lives. Wyeth himself became very ill and after sending the ship out half empty the men became discouraged.

Winter arrived, bringing with it rain, snow and ice. The river raged and the water rose higher and higher. The men were worn out, their horses had been stolen, and they were ready to quit.

Wyeth admitted defeat for good this time. Selling his business to the Hudson Bay Company, he departed Fort William in the spring of 1836 leaving one of the workers, Courtney Walker, in charge of the land.

After attempting to register the land in his name and failing, Wyeth gave up, and never returned.

Fort William faded into the landscape and farming has removed all traces of the town. However, Wyeth was ahead of the pack with his plans to capitalize on the potential of the Columbia River's annual salmon run. A true visionary, he blazed the trail for future businessmen and pioneers.

The overland route that he established eventually became the trail that brought tens of thousands of pioneer settlers westward. Huge caravans of covered wagons would follow his trail over the Blue Mountains to populate the northwest.

Although his business venture was unsuccessful, many of the men that Wyeth brought to Oregon remained to play an important part in local history. Some left their mark in small ways, like Thornburgh and Hubbard the men at the heart of Oregon's first trial, while others were instrumental in establishing ownership of this land by America and statehood for Oregon.

Courtney Walker, the man Wyeth left behind to watch over the island, joined up with a group sent west by the Mission Society of the Episcopal Church. They had come by ship to convert the Flathead Indians. Walker and these missionaries settled along the river where the natives were friendly.

They used Fort William as their temporary headquarters, while scouting the area for a more suitable mission location. The island itself was rejected because of its annual flooding. Ironically, the site that was eventually chosen, ten miles north of what is now Salem, flooded, while Wyeth's Fort William town site has never been covered with water.

These missionaries were led by Reverend Jason Lee and his nephew, Daniel Lee. Their group included two school teachers, Edwards and Shepard. Cyrus Shepard, a 23-year-old man from Kentucky ran a mission school, the first school south of the Columbia River, which makes him Oregon's first school teacher.

The mission they built north of Salem quickly became the center of American settlement for Oregon. Brought here by Wyeth, the Lees were the first missionaries to arrive. Their many religious accomplishments include preaching the first sermon west of the Rockies and holding the first religious funeral.

In 1837 when Jason Lee married Anna Maria Pittman they became the first white couple married in Oregon Country. Anna Pittman Lee also became the first white woman to die in Oregon.

Wyeth's missionaries played a big part in colonizing Oregon; they encouraged many to make the journey by sea to join them in their mission.

Before Jason Lee died in 1845 he turned his efforts toward establishing a government that would bring American control to Oregon. He petitioned Congress for protection for the settlers, promoted the first temperance society in the northwest, and helped to abolish slavery among the Indians.

Two scientists also accompanied Wyeth when he came west, Thomas Nuttall and J. K. Townsend. Nuttall was a botanist who studied the plants on the island; most had never been seen before by others in his profession. He spent his days identifying and categorizing the new species that he found.

Townsend was a naturalist; he studied birds. Just out of college, he declared the island to be his own little paradise. The Indians referred to him as the Bird Chief. He put together a huge collection of birds which were taken mostly from Sauvie Island.

Townsend also collected snakes, lizards and frogs in a two-gallon container he had filled with alcohol. Returning from an overnight journey he found a thirsty Thornburgh (the man who later became the subject of Oregon's first trial) had drunk up all of the alcohol, leaving his collection a useless mess.

This young naturalist was also determined to return to the East Coast with an Indian body wrapped for burial.

On the island he found what he thought to be the perfect specimen near Fort William. Wrapped in mats and placed in a canoe, the female remains rested in the branches of a tall tree. The flesh was dried and shriveled.

Quietly one night Townsend took a canoe to the burial location, removed his shoes, and crept to the tree where he stole the body. Upon returning to town he hid it, content that he had scored a centerpiece for his planned burial exhibit at the Academy of Natural Sciences in Philadelphia.

The next day the deceased young maiden's brother arrived on his annual pilgrimage to visit his sister's gravesite. Finding the body missing, and fresh shoe prints nearby, he hurried to Fort William to demand her return.

The distressed brother left the village carrying her dead body over his shoulder, wailing loudly over the loss of his sister and the type of people who would rob a burial site. Townsend returned to Philadelphia without his Indian burial exhibit.

Not long after Fort William was abandoned, an enterprising young man named Ewing Young moved onto the town site. Young had come to Fort Vancouver the same year Wyeth had arrived with his second expedition.

Penniless and half-starved, he had found the gate barred. McLoughlin had erroneously received word that Young was a horse thief, and orders had been issued to buy no furs from him and to give him no aid.

Unhappy with the treatment he received at the Hudson Bay Company while trying to make an honest living, Young decided to use Wyeth's deserted iron cauldrons to create a distillery.

Once used for pickling salmon, these pots were soon producing Tennessee whiskey. McLoughlin tried to put an end to this whiskey-making venture by offering to purchase the cauldrons, but Young refused his offer.

The missionaries were already having problems converting the Indians, and they too quickly came out against the making of liquor on Sauvie Island.

But, when the missionaries approached Young for the purpose of buying and destroying his business, they received an entirely different response. Not wanting to cause trouble, and having already gotten even with McLoughlin for treating him like a thief, Young gracefully abandoned everything without charge.

McLoughlin quickly took possession of the empty island. He had grown tired of the competition and problems going on so close to his headquarters. So, he came up with a plan to establish a dairy there, swimming the cattle across and down the river from Fort Vancouver.

Trading with the Russian settlement at Sitka with this in mind, McLoughlin offered butter in exchange for furs. He felt certain the island could easily support the cows necessary for this trade.

McLoughlin put a long-time Hudson Bay Company employee, Laurent Sauvé, in charge of this dairy. Four years later records show that the dairy operation had grown large enough to require three families to live on the island full time.

That first dairy was set up at the Fort William location; the second was located near Marquam Lake. This lake was named after the man who tended the lake's dairy herd.

In 1844 Laurent Sauvé retired as the dairy overseer and was succeeded by James and Isabelle Logie. This couple continued to operate the dairy for the Hudson Bay Company with the help of two men, James Taylor and Marquam, the dairy farmer near the lake.

In 1846, when the 49th parallel was established as the new United States boundary, the Hudson Bay Company gave up its island holdings and moved north.

That opened up the fertile land on Sauvie Island to homesteaders. The Logies and James Taylor stayed on the island, filing claims on the land they had managed for the Hudson Bay Company.

CHAPTER SIX

Sauvie Island
Oregon Territory Established and Island Settled

By 1819 Spain had relinquished all claims to the Oregon Territory. The Russians withdrew in 1825 and the British left in 1846, leaving the area open to homesteaders.

Early visitors had returned to the East with tales of an exciting young land, stirring the imagination of the adventurous, and creating a desire to move to the Pacific Northwest.

When 100 brave individuals made their way over the Oregon Trail in 1842, it marked the beginning of Oregon's settlement. To get there, these men and women travelled across vast areas inhabited only by Indians and wild animals.

Trappers and mountain men now led caravans of pioneers across the overland route, following the path opened by Wyeth.

Those early pioneers came in covered wagons, travelling just ten to twelve miles a day. Livestock accompanied the wagons and water was scarce; very few fresh provisions were available along the way. If you didn't bring it with you, you did without.

The trip was dangerous too. Wagons often broke down and the precious cargo carried had to be left behind. Stock wandered off and disappeared, and illness plagued the travelers.

The Indians were growing restless too, as the number of travelers increased and rain swollen streams left groups of settlers stranded near their villages for days.

Most of those travelers ended up in Oregon City, making a left turn at Sauvie Island to follow the Willamette River north past shores lined with woodlands. At the Willamette Falls where they stopped, those travelers built crude cabins and began to establish Oregon's seat of power.

Letters written by these settlers spoke of a great new territory, encouraging others to settle in Oregon. By 1847 more than 11,000 people had followed that 2,000 mile overland route to Oregon.

Like Wyeth, those early pioneers believed a great city would someday exist at the head of Oregon's navigable waters. Settlers tried to outguess their neighbors, hoping to find themselves in the right spot when it happened.

In 1848 Oregon was established as a U.S. territory. This new Oregon Territory included all of Washington and parts of Idaho, Montana and Wyoming.

The building of Portland had begun and the town now contained six buildings. Populations were also increasing quickly in the towns of Milwaukie and Linnton.

Late in 1850 Congress passed the Donation Land Law to encourage pioneers to endure the hardship of settling a new land. This Land Law required the registry of all land titles showing clearly marked property lines.

Free land was available to any man over 18 years of age who registered their claim before December 1, 1855. A single man could claim 320 acres of land, while a married man was entitled to twice that amount with half belonging to his wife.

Many men arrived in the Pacific Northwest without a wife, but with the prospect of acquiring twice as much land, marriage quickly became desirable.

At that time men in the Oregon Territory outnumbered women nine to one. In order to get around the law, adult men often married girls eleven to thirteen years old so that they could acquire more land. These young brides generally stayed with their families until older, while the man who had become their husband worked the land.

The settling of Sauvie Island was no different. Young men and couples arrived ready to begin a new life, and to lay claim to the free land. Many of their descendants still have island ties.

Sauvie Island settlers, like Wyeth, believed this island would one day become that great shipping terminus, and the location of a major city.

James and Isabelle Logie staked their claim to the dairy site where they had toiled for the Hudson Bay Company. Isabelle Logie is thought to be the first white woman to travel the Oregon Trail; area Indians called her the White Godmother because she doctored them when they were ill.

Before his death in 1854 Isabelle's husband James helped to transform the Indian trail leading over the Tualatin Mountains into an important trade route. Known as the Logie Trail, it connects the Willamette and Tualatin Valleys together.

The Logies had no children during their fourteen-year marriage. After the death of her husband Isabelle Logie married Jonathan Moar and they had six children. With that marriage the Logie claim became known as the Moar-Logie Claim. The Moars have descendants who still call the island home.

James Taylor, another former Hudson Bay Company dairy employee, also returned to stake his claim on the island. He too chose high ground along the channel side of the island. His land claim later became the site of the island's first post office. Known as the Arthur Post Office, it was in continuous operation for twenty-four years.

Alexander McQuinn, Martin Gillihan, Matthew White, Leonard Jewett and William Cooper also posted their claims on this fertile island. Like Wyeth and the Indians before them, each chose a cleared meadow or burned-over ground. This saved months of hard work; without having to clear trees they could quickly begin plowing the land and planting crops.

Over half of the original island settlers came from Missouri, including James Cline and his wife. The Clines soon became parents to the first island-born American child.

The Reeder name is also still a familiar one on the island. Simon Reeder, along with his wife and four-year-old son, left Indiana in 1853. After travelling to The Dalles by oxen, they loaded their possessions onto a raft and rode the swift waters of the Columbia downriver.

The Reeders, like all of the other early travelers, were forced to portage five miles around the waterfalls at the present Bonneville Dam site before taking their final raft ride down the Columbia. When the family came to Sauvie Island they beached their crude craft and brought an end to the seven month journey; they had found their new home.

Choosing one of the empty Indian village sites, the Reeders were forced to deal with the devastation of the sickness that had killed the island Indians. The Reeder family removed hundreds of human bones and skulls; these were hauled away by the wheelbarrow loads as they cleared the land for plowing. They did this surrounded by Indian burial canoes cradled in the tree branches.

Simon Reeder, a skilled carpenter, soon erected a warm and cozy cabin for his young family. The first Reeder homes were carried away by high water; they learned where to build and had better luck as the years went on. The Reeders still occupy a portion of their original land claim.

The Morgan family settled on Sauvie Island in 1849, building their first home on a high rise of ground as was the custom by then. They built a big house in 1883, which survived all of the island's floods, including the big one that took so much in 1894.

That year the water got three feet deep on the first floor, and the lower outbuildings were entirely wrecked, but the house survived. That big house survived 67 years of high water, but fire finally triumphed where water could not, destroying the house in 1950.

Five single males came to stake their claims on the island; Ellis Walker, James Menzies, Horace McIntire, Joseph Charlton and James Bybee all arrived in search of free land. Marriage would double their allowable claim, and one father stepped up offering to provide wives for all five of the men.

While other island settlers were totally isolated from their kin, with relatives living thousands of miles away, with this move the Miller girls would be surrounded by family. These five families built their homes as close to each other as their land claims allowed.

One of those unmarried men, James Bybee, had arrived on the island already a rich man. After becoming one of the three original Multnomah County Commissioners, he began the construction of a stately family home on Sauvie Island.

Sitting atop a rise of high ground, the house was designed to look out over the channel toward the mountains beyond. It was the first plaster house built in Oregon; the materials were brought by ship from New York, around Cape Horn.

The house had nine rooms; seven of those rooms had fireplaces to drive out the chill of the damp Oregon climate. The bricks for these fireplaces were made on the east side of the island.

In 1858 the Bybee family left the house and land claim behind, heading off in search of greener pastures. Dr. Benjamin Howell, who had settled the parcel of land adjoining the Bybee land claim, purchased the house and moved his family into the handsome two-story building.

The Howell family was anti-slavery and had come west in search of a place where they could raise their children away its cruelty. The year before their island purchase Oregon

Territory inhabitants had voted to ban slavery. This landslide victory had a final count of three to one.

One of the Howell boys, Thomas, grew up to become a pioneer botanist. Along with his brother Joseph, he collected and cataloged most of the plant life for this part of the U.S.

Howell's catalogs were originally put together for the purpose of selling collections of pressed specimens, seeds, bulbs and plants and were sent all over America and Europe.

More than 2,000 of his specimens are still being held by the Chicago Museum of Natural History, another 3,000 at a conservatory in Switzerland, and the University of Oregon has 10,000 of Howell's island specimens.

The Bybee house remained in the Howell family until 1961, when it was purchased by Multnomah County. Restored to showcase 19th Century farm life in Oregon Territory, it was designated a National Historical Landmark and became known as the Bybee-Howell House.

The Bybee-Howell grounds offer a quiet retreat into the past. You'll find 93-acre Howell Park behind the house; it is operated by Metro Parks and Greenspaces. This park includes an heirloom pioneer orchard, rose garden, picnic tables and trails leading to Howell Lake wetlands.

When this book was first released the Bybee-Howell House was authentically furnished with period antiques and could be toured by visitors. It is currently closed, but the grounds are still open to the public.

Sauvie Island's original settlers came from all walks of life. Most were farmers, or raised livestock, but others had worked at various trades before arriving on the island.

These first settlers built their homes on small knolls, either natural or man-made, to avoid the high water. Sometimes, when high land was not available island homes were built on stilts. The sheds and outbuildings too had to be planned for the rising river. Barns were often built on pilings and extended over the water.

Those first houses were built quickly; most had a dirt floor and were just one or two rooms. A large fireplace used for cooking and warmth would have monopolized one end. The whole family lived, ate and slept in these cramped quarters. As time passed, island families were able to build bigger, more permanent homes.

Most of those larger island homes were clapboard buildings with a porch on two or more sides. In 1893 one island family built their home of bricks; the entire house, including basement walls and foundation, were made of brick. Its construction required more than 180,000 bricks, all of which were made right on the island.

Settlers arrived with cattle, horses, sheep and hogs, but adding more livestock once you were here was nearly impossible. Hunting had to supply meat for the table so that the livestock could be left to multiply.

Although island farmers knew all about the latest farming methods, getting started was difficult in the late 1800's. Seeds were scarce and tools were crude; markets were non-existent so there was no incentive to produce large crops.

Producing more food than your family required was a lot of extra work. Wheat had to be sown by hand and harvested the same way. Mowing was done with a scythe and the grain was then thrashed using livestock.

Island families quickly learned that the fertile soil would grow a wider variety of plants than the dry earth of the plains they had left behind. They planted fruit trees and vegetables, and watched them flourish in the rich black dirt.

Large families were common among pioneer families and the children were expected to help with the work. The girls often cared for younger siblings while helping with the housework and the boys worked the land.

After all, an unending supply of butter needed to be churned, you made your own soap in boiling pots, clothing was washed by hand, and food had to be canned and stored for the winter. That kept the women and girls pretty busy.

Young boys often started out weeding the garden and caring for livestock. Before long they were helping to plow the fields, bringing in the hay, and hunting fresh meat for the table. Maturing early, children were often married by age 15.

Scarcely anything was purchased. A spinning wheel and loom generally occupied one corner of even the tiniest cabin. Here, yarn was spun and woven into cloth. The cloth then had to be hand-dyed before the family's clothing could be made. Idle time was unheard of in those days.

Reading was a popular family activity on the island, but most homes only possessed two volumes; the Bible and the works of William Shakespeare. It was from these books that children generally got their only look at the world beyond the island. Outside, their immediate world was bound by a wall of timber that began just beyond the clearing, and a river that ran past their doorstep.

In 1848 gold was discovered at Sutters Fort, California. Nearly two-thirds of all men living in Oregon immediately rushed south to the gold fields, including men from the island. They left their wives and children behind to struggle with the harvest as best they could, and island families proved to be more than capable of the task.

While the men were trying to wash fortunes from the California river beds, their families were capitalizing on the need for food that had been created by the gold rush.

Everything available was shipped south to feed the hordes that had descended on the gold fields from all directions. Island families were soon bringing in more money with one harvest than the men had made in all of the years they had spent farming the land.

Some men returned wealthy, which increased the demand for store-bought goods. Families were now leaving the land to build homes in town; some with plans to open a business. This made growing food for others a viable Oregon business.

In less than two years nearby Portland went from just a few buildings to a bustling community with more than 250 houses and 18 shops. People living in town brought an increased need for store-bought milk, fresh vegetables and farm products, and the islanders stepped in to sell those items to city dwellers.

Dairy and truck farming quickly became a huge island industry. Milk and butter were sent to the city, along with vegetables, beef and pork.

Island ranchers have always sold their cows right after the summer flooding was over, after first allowing the herd to graze the fertile lowlands. Before the next flood could overtake those low pastures, all of the cattle had to be sold.

The lure of free land was successful in bringing people westward. After the original Donation Land Law expired in 1855 migration began to slow down since land was no longer free. People continued to come west and settle on Sauvie Island but they staked out much smaller claims.

The island was still a long way from being civilized. Deer, small wildlife, and an occasional cougar or bear were often sighted. Ducks and geese were plentiful too, but the city offered no market for waterfowl.

One enterprising islander shot the birds and used them to feed his hogs. After all, there was a good market for bacon, even if no one wanted to buy the ducks and geese.

Indians still frequented the island, living by their own rules. It was not uncommon for them to help themselves to the settlers' property. By their way of thinking they were fair about it; for as long as the Indian had been around for the island's harvests they had never withheld the bounty from anyone.

With this in mind, the Indians took what they needed from the pioneer crops and considered it fair. An island family might find that their rifle had disappeared, but it would soon be returned, along with a portion of the game that had been killed with the gun.

In those days the only way to reach Sauvie Island was by water. Riverfront claims all had their own dock where steam ships unloaded passengers, parcels and livestock.

A trip to Portland was hectic and filled with excitement. Errands had to be run and purchases made, all before the return ship arrived to be boarded. Returning home, passengers sometimes shared the deck not only with their purchases, but also with a herd of cattle bound for the island.

Even though the island got its own post office in 1851 receiving mail was still uncertain. Mail from the East Coast or Midwest went through San Francisco first, before it came by water up the Pacific coastline.

Mail was left at the most convenient location, regardless of where the post office was located. Extra stops were discouraged, and the family with the largest delivery often received every item intended for the island on their dock.

Since no roads crossed the island, communicating with your neighbor meant walking or travelling by horseback. Crossing fields and climbing fences was the only way to shorten the distance. In calm weather it was often easier to make the journey by boat. Because of this, families often remained isolated for long periods of time.

That isolation went on for a very long time; it would be decades before roads would cross the island. And, those first roads were nothing more than wagon ruts leading over high ground, but at least a route had been established.

A permanent, full-time ferry would not be brought to the island until after the turn of the century. And, it would be more than a hundred years after the arrival of those first island pioneers before a bridge was built, connecting Sauvie Island to the mainland. Until then the islanders enjoyed relative isolation.

Many of the island's early landowners were happy to see civilization delayed, and some fought right up to the very end to keep their island accessible only by water.

This group of island residents was against the building of roads that would connect their homes as well, but in time the island's more progressive inhabitants would win both battles.

Sauvie Island; A Step Back in Time

CHAPTER SEVEN

How the Rising Water Affected Island Life

On the island there used to be a saying: *"You can always spot a newcomer by the way he talks about the high water."* Old-timers still regard the high water as annual freshets; a new resident talks about the flooding.

Sauvie Island was originally formed by water. For centuries the Columbia and Willamette Rivers have joined together here, against a ledge of stone located near the present site of Warrior Rock, on the downriver end of the island.

This stone ledge caused the water to slow its pace, and as it slowed it dumped its load of fertile silt. In time this dumping action built up, and the island became high land. The ever-moving water kept this land in a state of constant change, washing it away in one place, building it up in another.

Today, man-made dikes and jetties, along with diligent river dredging, keep the shoreline predictable. Before the dikes, jetties and dredging, the annual high water was looked upon as a normal part of island lifestyle.

Twice a year island families simply had to be ready to leave their homesteads, taking with them everything of value that couldn't be put out of the water's reach.

The first rising freshet happened during early summer, when the river was swollen with melting snow. Late each fall the water would rise again, when a sudden stretch of warm weather melted the early snow upriver. The rising waters from snow-swollen rivers were often made worse by heavy rain.

Some years the residents would simply move to the upper story of their homes, and watch the water as it passed over the land and through the first floor of the house.

If they chose to move upstairs, they had to take with them everything lying within the grasp of that swirling water; anything that wasn't removed or securely fastened down would be carried away.

Small animals were often made secure in barn lofts or attics, but the larger livestock always had to be moved. Generally the move was a short one, relocating livestock to the island's higher ground until the flooding had passed.

At other times those rising waters meant transporting all of the livestock across the river channel, to a place where the land was considerably higher.

Occasionally a stray cow would get caught on the island with nowhere to go, drowning where it stood, generally on the highest ground it could find.

Because of this most island livestock, with the exception of dairy stock, was generally sold each spring, saving the farmers all of the extra work they would cause during high water.

Many early residents believed the annual rise in the river did more good than it did harm. After all, once those June freshets had come and gone, the land would retain the rich topsoil carried from upstream.

As each small creek and stream upriver had overflowed, it had grabbed the fertile earth lodged along its banks. Carried downriver by the bigger rivers, when that rush of water encountered the stone barrier of Warrior Rock, most of that fertile soil was dumped.

Each year when the high water receded it left the land dotted with tiny pools. These were often filled with small salmon, bass, sunfish, perch, catfish, trout and crappies.

The heat from the warm summer sun would rapidly evaporate the water, and those young fish would perish, adding their bodies to the natural compost of the land.

Early in the twentieth century island families began to scoop those fish before the water could disappear. Hundreds of thousands of small fish were gathered on the island and shipped out every year. These ended up in barren ponds and large lakes all across the state.

Wading waist deep in the mud the island men would draw their nets through the water, often from sun up to sun down. During one five-year period more than 16 million fish were netted.

This island operation is what initially stocked Oregon waters with its abundance of fish; many of which were not normally encountered in western lakes until that time.

In June of 1894 the water reached a height of 33 feet, flooding all but the highest land along the channel. This flood killed two 125-year-old fir trees. Since fir will not survive high water it is safe to assume that this was the highest water since before 1769, and maybe longer.

When the water finally receded, the remaining buildings were filled with mud and the overflow had carried debris through fences and scattered it all over the island.

During the early 1900's several flood control acts were drawn up by the U.S. government. Population growth, along with the cutting of timber on high land, had increased flood damage drastically and the government was looking for a way to control the situation.

Some island residents were completely against building dikes or levees on the island. They believed man had no right to alter the course of nature. They asked ... *"What right did they have to turn the tiny lakes and wet lowland into dry, farmable soil?"*

Many more residents argued for the creation of safe, yet fertile farmland. They wanted the peace of mind that would allow them to work their land to its fullest, without being at the whim of the rising water.

With adequate dikes, these residents believed their crops would never again be washed away, nor would the livestock need to be sold early to remove them from the flood endangered land.

In 1921 the landowners living near the lower end of the island voted to have a 21-mile-long dike built to protect 4,000 acres from the rapid runoff. A macadam highway ran along the top;

a road that would sit high above the water for most of the year.

This small dike protected the land well until 1933 when 1600 acres of crops were destroyed as the water broke through its protective barrier near the head of Willow Bar Slough.

A 75-foot-wide crack in the dike allowed the Columbia River to pour through at a perilous pace. Water rose 18" a day over some of the best farms in the state.

Ten island families stood by helplessly as their entire alfalfa and wheat crops disappeared. Most of the livestock had been removed from the island and sold, and smaller animals were housed on the upper floors of homes and outbuildings where their owners hoped to insure their survival.

But that was not enough during that fateful 1933 rise of the river, and the residents who had remained behind eventually climbed out of their upper story windows onto barges brought in for their rescue. It took six weeks for the water to go down.

Five years later another break occurred in that same dike. The swollen river seeped through, washing soil away until less than six feet remained to hold the water back.

Island families struggled day and night for four long days doing everything they could to reinforce a 500' stretch of dike that was slowly disintegrating. Men, women and children relentlessly filled burlap bags with sand, and stuffed those, along with tons of hay, into the holes.

Because ships continued to travel the river the Islander's efforts were washed away time after time when the swells created as they passed emptied the cracks faster than they could refill them with sandbags.

Reeder Road remained above water in only a few spots, leaving thirteen families and 1500 head of livestock dependent on watercraft for their rescue and evacuation.

Just as they were ready to leave, the river reached its crest and the water level began to drop. The battle was over and the residents could stay.

In 1936 the Federal Flood Control Act was passed to help build dikes and levees all across the United States. After that second flood most of the island's southern property owners agreed to allow the government to build a dike to protect their 12,000 acres.

This dike was designed in a manner that allowed farming to be done right up to the top, and the landowners agreed to handle all maintenance once it was completed.

In 1940 Congress approved a $1,763,000 budget and once the rivers had passed their summer crest, three shifts of men started work on the new 18' wide dike. Heavy equipment was ferried in and put to work 24 hours a day.

Those men and machines worked furiously to construct more than 19 miles of pile and rock dikes before the water once again rose to threaten the land.

Known as The Big Dike, it cut off one end of the Gilbert River. A canal had to be dug to lead the Gilbert River along the inside of the new dike and into a pumping plant. This was done to provide the island interior with controlled drainage.

An operator would now be able to raise and lower the interior water table to relieve the stress from a river that was trying to pass though the absorbent land beneath the island's surface to seek its own level inside.

Little Sturgeon, Mouse and Marquam Lakes began to dry up. This dike had not only altered the face of the island, but it also reclaimed land long covered by water. Barren lake beds reverted to state ownership and were offered for sale.

The photo on the preceding page shows how little of the land remains above water during flooding.

In 1948 another big flood came, threatening The Big Dike, and once again island residents prepared for evacuation. The water continued to rise until families within the lower dike were forced to leave as the water came rushing over the top.

During that 1948 flood residents could only sit by helplessly watching as farms inside the smaller dike flooded when the dike washed away. Sand bags and reinforcements were continually added to the new dike in an attempt to stop the oncoming flow from travelling across the remaining acres.

Worried that the dikes would break, families living on the southern half of the island were asked to leave their farms and move to higher land.

Cows were once again marched out of their barns, and loaded onto barges before they could be washed away.

Furniture had to be moved to the upper levels of island homes, small animals were housed and tended in barn lofts, the dike was watched 24 hours a day, and island farmers now had to add a twice-a-day journey to the mainland in order to do their milking.

These flood photographs show the 1948 evacuation of the Hutchinson Ranch. Cattle are being marched onto a barge for the ride to the mainland, leaving behind a farm where water was quickly covering the barns and outbuildings.

More than 250 soldiers and volunteers were brought to the island to help fight the rising water. They came from the mainland, riding the Burlington Ferry which was forced to abandon its 38-year-old route in order to reach high land.

Those men arrived in cattle trucks, on a ferry that wound its way between trees until it found a high spot beside the Sauvie Island Road where they could disembark.

Eventually the river reached its peak, just two feet short of The Big Dike's full height, and a full 15 feet above flood stage. But, the river's cresting didn't mark the end of danger. For several weeks the water level remained high, and it continued to soak through the dike in many places.

When the residents were finally able to return to their homes they were faced with mud and muck inside all of the buildings. Although the houses had been built with high water in mind, the river had crept over doorsills and the flooded land was left barren.

Returning livestock found no pasture, nor was there any hay to be cut for winter feed. The island residents felt the effects of that flooding for a long time, even though they had managed to come though it without the loss of human life.

Since then the annual freshets have been kinder. The Big Dike provides protection to the majority of island residents while two smaller dikes protect the lower end.

But water didn't always bring trouble; the river also brought an ever-changing view as first rafts and canoes, and then later sailing vessels, sternwheelers and steamers passed within view.

The sound of a whistle would signal the arrival of a boat which often stopped at several landings to pick up milk and butter on its way to town.

In the 1870's a flat-bottomed grocery boat made regular trips around the island. Operated with sails and oars, the Frenchman and his helper who ran it made a fourteen day journey around the island's edge, selling bulk goods, cloth, dried fish and matches to the residents.

The children were not forgotten either; he brought peppermint candy sticks to hand out on arrival. Everyone looked forward to the arrival of the grocery boat.

Because Sauvie Island sits along the route to Portland, now one of the west coast's largest harbors, ocean vessels constantly glide past island homes.

When the fog gets thick, as it so often does near the river, these ships are sometimes entirely invisible from shore. The blast of their whistles, as they signal each other, is both a comforting and haunting sound.

The river also brings salmon and sturgeon fishing to the island. A boat is not necessary; fishermen can stand along the shore and try their hand at snagging these tasty fish. Long stretches of quiet sandy beaches lie outside the protective dikes; many are accessible to visiting anglers.

During the summer Sauvie Island beaches are filled with people who yearn for the seaside, yet don't want to make a two-hour drive to find clouds on the other side of the mountains.

Because of its low water table the island is dotted with lakes. They sport names like Racetrack, Millionaire, Crane and Mud Lake; each tells its own story about island history.

Racetrack Lake was named because it is thought to be the location of Indian horse races held during annual fairs. Other lakes carry the names of people, ducks, fish, fowl, trees, meadows and shapes. The settlers' imaginations seemed to be the only limit when naming island lakes.

The largest is called Sturgeon Lake, and it's a place where Indian legend tells us giant sturgeon came to rest. Early pioneer tales claim that fish found within this big lake were so large that nightfall would find them reaching up to strip bark from the trees. Since the addition of the dike, the water level has been kept low enough to keep bark-eating creatures at bay.

Over the years the rocks off Warrior Point have proven to be a hazard to vessels. In 1888 the Warrior Rock Lighthouse was built to call attention to those dangerous rocks. A 34-year-old fog bell, removed from the Cape Disappointment Lighthouse in 1881, was installed the following year. This bell warned boaters of the rocky danger from 1889 to 1961.

The original 1889 two-story wooden lighthouse was small, and sat on a square sandstone base. In the 1930s a new lighthouse with a 28-foot concrete tower was built.

But, even with a lighthouse and bell in place, ships still crashed into the point. The *Manzanita*, the same ship that had been used to install the new lighthouse, ran afoul of the point 18 years later, causing it to sink in just a few minutes.

In 1939 the U.S. Coast Guard took over the lighthouse, installing their keeper in a large white house overlooking the river. Living in isolation, he would row a boat over to St. Helens when in need of supplies or mail.

But all of this was brought to an end when a tugboat towing an empty steel barge lost its tow, and the lighthouse structure was completely destroyed.

The Coast Guard sent a ship out to remove the old bell from the collapsing structure, and in the process it crashed through the deck, breaking off a portion of the bell and causing severe damage.

You can see the old bell at the front entrance to the Columbia County Courthouse in St. Helens.

CHAPTER EIGHT

Time Brings Changes
and a Bridge to the Mainland

Although the force of water, and man's fight to hold that water back, brought many changes to the island time brought even more.

When those original sixteen families staked their land claims only a small portion of the island was occupied. The lack of roads and great distances between the homesteads kept each family a separate unit.

Even after a market for their farm goods had been established in Portland, and the steamboat made daily stops to pick up dairy products, most island families remained isolated. The land supplied most of their needs and for some families that was reason enough to stay home.

By then the Multnomah Channel had become a busy waterway. Although called the Willamette Slough by those who travelled its waters, this is the same channel that Broughton named Calls River, Lewis & Clark referred to as Wapato Inlet, and Wilkes dubbed Warrior Branch.

Boats bustling up and down the channel that separated Sauvie Island from the mainland had names like *Young America, Columbia, Lot Whitcomb, Francis-Alice* and *Lucea Mason*. Some were on regular routes; one boat travelled from Milwaukee to Astoria, another ran from Astoria to Portland, and there was a daily boat between Portland and St. Helens.

Steamboats chugged upstream with passengers standing on deck, enjoying the beauty of the Tualatin Mountains to the west and the low timber covered flatlands of Sauvie Island to the east.

At least six boat landings sat along the island's channel banks, and if passengers or goods were waiting the boats might stop at all six on a busy day.

The Columbia River side of the island provided its residents with an entirely different type of boat to watch, the large ocean-going sailing ship. They also took a different boat into Portland than neighbors 5 miles across the island.

Each side of the island had its own post office as well. Facing what is now the state of Washington, the Columbia River post office was known as the Mouth of the Willamette Post Office or Sauvies. The Channel post office was called Arthur.

The Arthur postmistress was one of the Taylor children, Mary. She named it using the first name of the man who had authorized its existence.

The island's dairy farmers started two granges around 1874. Early membership was divided fairly evenly between the two, with one group representing the republican farmers and the other the democrats.

Because a grange operates to help the farmer, and not the politician, this division was later dropped with the formation of the Sauvie Island Grange; one group dedicated to serving all farmers regardless of their political affiliation.

Sauvie Island; A Step Back in Time

Over a 100-year time span Sauvie Island had a number of small ferries that took people back and forth across the channel. Multnomah County established a regular ferry service in 1911, providing island access to the state's first big road paving project at Burlington.

That first ferry was wooden. Known as the *Burlington Ferry*, it was small, and residents spent a lot of time waiting for it to arrive. It was later replaced by a 16-car steel ferry that served the island until the bridge was built in 1950.

Those first ferry boat operators had lots of time on their hands for fishing, but before the ferry was retired they were transporting up to 1500 cars in a single day, and nobody had any spare time. Ferry service ran from 5:30 a.m. until 1:00 a.m. the following day.

In 1912 two St. Helens brothers, Hamlin and Charles McCormick, extended their lumber and shipping holdings across the river to the lower end of Sauvie Island. Creating a 1,000 acre industrial area, these men brought jobs to the island.

Wooden steam schooners were built here, and each one needed a crew of 70 for construction. The first boat completed, the *Multnomah*, caused a big local sensation.

Its launch attracted two steamships from Portland and another from Astoria, each packed with people who had come just to watch the boat being launched. Several hundred people were there for the christening, a huge crowd for that time.

With an overall length of 216', the *Multnomah* was large enough to carry one million board feet of lumber while supplying accommodations for 60 passengers. It was built to travel between the mainland and Hawaii.

The launching of the *Wapama* in 1915 didn't create the excitement of that first ship; after all it was just one among many by then. The *Wapama* however, carried lumber to California, returning with goods needed by the settlers, which made it an extremely important ship for Oregonians.

For decades the *Wapama* was part of a historic ship exhibit at the San Francisco Maritime Museum. At that time it had been restored to its original state, and was featured as one of the few remaining wooden steam schooners in the world. It now sits in a museum dry dock waiting for another restoration.

The island shipbuilding operation ended when steel ships began to replace those made of wood. But, the boats built on Sauvie Island went on to travel west coast waters for a long, long time.

During prohibition liquor raids were happening on the mainland all around the island; a number of stills were discovered between Linnton and St. Helens.

It seems unlikely that a place as inaccessible as Sauvie Island, with its small population and unwatched lands, would have escaped the eye of the distiller. Supplies and output could have come and gone by boat undetected, and island stories say it did.

By 1931 there were 250 families living on the island. Their children attended school at one of four locations; some schools were taught in small antiquated schoolhouses while others were located in the homes of large families.

In 1932 a modern public school was built and within five years all of the other schools had closed their doors.

This school educated island children until January of 1979 when it burned to the ground. A new school was built in 1980; it served K-8. High school students have always attended school on the mainland.

With 2011 enrollment barely over 200, the old school was closed. It has since reopened as Sauvie Island Academy, a charter school, which means students from outside the district can attend as well.

Electricity was not available to all island homes until 1938. Prior to that only those families living next to the power line that ran out to the lighthouse were able to get electric service. Because of its sparse population the electric company was reluctant to install more lines.

To overcome those reservations island farmers worked together to show the electric company why they should provide service to the entire island.

Property owners donated right-of-way to their land; they trimmed trees, and calculated the electrical needs for each family. By doing all of this, they proved to the electric company that a profit was possible, and the entire island got power.

In 1936 the island saw its first newspaper. An outgrowth of an experimental agricultural station, the *Island Wapato* covered only what news the editor thought would be of interest to residents, along with agricultural reports. Its publication was sporadic at best, and it ceased altogether in 1941.

Seventy-two years after its invention, the first telephone was installed on Sauvie Island. Isolation had now gone the way of kerosene lamps and gasoline-operated water pumps. However, party lines were still in use on the island until the late 1970s.

After construction of The Big Dike island farmers began to switch over from dairy farming to the growing of row crops. During World War II, when most young men were away at war, one island farmer used prisoners and parolees to work his 830 acre farm. This gave minor offenders the opportunity to learn new skills while working in the fresh air.

Because he offered legitimate employment, and the city had no work farms of their own at that time, local judges happily supplied him with plenty of labor. This war-born experiment was responsible for the creation of a controlled parole system, and the position of parole officer for the municipal court.

Most resident didn't like the idea of having convicts on the island so as soon as the war was over this practice was stopped.

Ferry service was offered for decades, but it was not always reliable. A ferry breakdown meant only people with boats could reach or leave the island, and in the winter it was not uncommon to find the channel full of ice. During some years ice brought traffic on the Columbia and Willamette Rivers to a screeching halt as well.

When the Multnomah Channel froze solid the islanders could walk to the mainland. Some years the ice got thick enough to drive on, and island farmers could motor their dairy products across the river to waiting trucks.

If the ice was not thick enough to withstand the weight of vehicles, human chains would be formed between the channel banks and they would slide the milk cans across.

The ferry landing provided access to the four-mile county road that ran along the west shore. Except for a two mile extension that went east, there were no other roads on the island back then.

Reaching the ferry landing for some residents meant driving cattle or hauling freight across open fields. Gates along the way allowed them to cross their neighbor's land, and many gates needed to be opened and closed before the ferry landing was reached. But, most of the island residents liked it that way.

Some residents, however, were convinced that the lack of roads was making their lives unbearable.

In 1915 those residents submitted a petition asking for the construction of a new road on the island. One family had already erected a small bridge across Dairy Creek, on the east side. The proposed road would utilize this, and extend the county road across the island to travel along the Columbia River.

Five days after the petition was filed a flood of protests poured in; these claimed that no roads were necessary, and pointed out that there was only one proper way to travel the island, and that was by boat. This group even wanted the bridge across Dairy Creek wiped off the map.

Many raised the objection that the building of roads would mean the confiscation of private property, and the island became the site of an old fashioned Kentucky-style feud, which caused the original petition to be thrown out of court.

This matter was eventually appealed all the way to the Supreme Court before a road was allowed to be built.

In 1923 the island mindset had changed some, but not enough. When Portland decided to replace the Burnside Bridge a delegation from Sauvie Island was sent to speak with the County Commissioners about the cost and advisability of moving part of that bridge to the Multnomah Channel.

Preliminary plans were drawn up to float the span downriver where it was to be located a short distance from the Willamette, connecting Sauvie Island to the mainland.

But, once again the island property owners were divided; some insisted the bridge belonged near the ferry landing. Unable to agree in time, the bridge was lost to another buyer.

By not acting together the residents lost out; 27 years later it would cost nearly ten times what they would have paid in 1923 to erect an island bridge.

One ferry was not enough either; it was not unusual for 1500 cars to use the Burlington Ferry during a typical summer Sunday, making it necessary to hire four pilots.

Although Portland now had several new bridges, some of the most fertile land in Oregon still relied on transportation so primitive that island children had to be boarded in town if their parents wanted them to have a high school education.

It was those Sunday drivers, along with repeated appeals from dairy operators and farmers, that soon brought graded rock roads to the island.

The first Sauvie Island Bridge was installed in 1950. Designed and built by the State Highway Commission, island residents were tired of fighting and left all decisions up to them.

Residents could no longer endure hours of waiting for an overcrowded ferry, or for the repair of a broken ferry cable. Residents and visitors could now come and go on their own schedule.

This first 1200' steel span bridge was supported by three concrete piers, with the center form resting on bedrock found 63' below the water's surface. The last 28 feet were drilled through mud and clay before a solid surface was finally located.

At a cost of slightly less than $1 million, the bridge connecting Sauvie Island to the mainland not only offered convenience, it meant lives would be saved during sickness, fires and floods.

However, nothing lasts forever and cracks were discovered in that bridge in 2001. In the final days of 2007 a $38 million tied-arch bridge span made its way down the Willamette River to Sauvie Island.

It travelled supported in midair, hovering over the barge, while a team of tug boats controlled its every movement. After much work the bridge was opened in June of 2008; the total cost was $43 million. The old bridge was scrapped.

In spite of numerous appeals to subdivide this fertile farmland it has remained primarily agricultural. When the first edition of this book was published the island population was less than half of what it was when Lewis and Clark estimated the native population. Thirty years later it remains the same, and consists of both land and water-based residents.

Because Sauvie Island provides an oasis of fresh air and country fun only a short distance from downtown Portland the visitors sometimes outnumber residents by 100 to 1 during the summer.

City dwellers come to the island to sunbathe, pick fresh vegetables and berries, bicycle, fish, hunt, canoe and relax!

CHAPTER NINE

The Sauvie Island Wildlife Management Area

As World War II drew to a close the Oregon Wildlife Commission initiated a plan to purchase the northern portion of Sauvie Island. This seven member board wanted the land preserved and developed as a refuge for wintering waterfowl. Thanks to them half the island is now state owned.

The majority of this land is within the Sauvie Island Wildlife Management Area (SIWA). Operated by the Oregon Department of Fish and Wildlife (ODFW), this refuge provides habitat for waterfowl, conserves the island's natural resources, and offers recreational and hunting opportunities to the public.

Every Wildlife Area visitor will need a parking permit if they plan on getting out of their cars inside the wildlife area. Parking permits are $7 for a one day pass or $22 for an annual permit. Parking permits are available at all island stores, Oregon Fish and Wildlife offices, and from ODFW agents.

Sauvie Island is located along the Pacific Flyway, the migratory bird route between Alaska and South America, and host to more than 150,000 waterfowl every day during the migration season.

More than 274 bird species have been spotted on the island, plus 37 different mammals and 13 herptiles. Island lakes harbor both resident and migratory fish, and thousands of shorebirds visit the island each year making it a great place for birdwatchers and hikers.

Waterfowl is so plentiful during the migratory period that on one day 120,000 waterfowl were counted on Sturgeon Lake alone. To encourage wintering waterfowl they plant 1200 acres of corn, millet and buckwheat every year. Deer, song birds, and other island wildlife benefit as well.

Sturgeon Lake, at 2,928 acres, is the largest island lake; it sits in the center of Sauvie Island. Connected to a maze of smaller floodplain lakes, the water level of this and all other island lakes are influenced by the ocean tides.

Boat access to Sturgeon Lake can be gained from the Multnomah Channel through the Gilbert River. Bird watching, hiking, canoeing, fishing and seasonal hunting are all popular Sturgeon Lake activities.

The Sauvie Island Wildlife Management Area provides duck and goose hunting opportunities September thru January. The area is divided into three units – Eastside, Westside and North. Hunters are required to purchase and carry a SIWA hunting permit within these areas. All Oregon Fish and Wildlife rules apply as well as those specific to Sauvie Island.

Sauvie Island hunting permits are available only on hunt days and the number of permits handed out varies based on each unit's quantity and type of blinds, topography, hunter demand, waterfowl distribution and other factors. Two of the hunting blinds are reserved for people with a disabled hunter permit and are wheelchair accessible.

If you're interested in hunting stop at the SIWA information office on Sauvie Island Road and ask for a copy of their Guide to Waterfowl Hunting on Sauvie Island. It has detailed maps and complete details on each hunting area. The staff can also familiarize you with island fishing regulations.

The rivers hold salmon, steelhead, cutthroat trout and sturgeon; island lakes offer perch, catfish, bass, bluegill and crappie. Prior to the building of the dikes there were 88 lakes on the island. There are fewer lakes now, but the fishing is still good.

Sauvie Island is a perfect place for easy hiking too, but you need to bring your own water, pack out all garbage, and be prepared for primitive restrooms.

The land is flat and there are lots of gravel maintenance roads that provide easy walking. Unless otherwise marked, all SIWA roads are open for hiking. You'll find lots of little trails along these roads too, presenting opportunities for further exploration.

The Sauvie Island Wildlife Management Area has four public beaches; all are situated along the Columbia River. In total, they cover 112 acres and provide lots of sandy beach space.

Most of these beaches sit outside the man-made dike; staircases have been constructed along the dike for easy access. Parking is plentiful, but you'll need to purchase a parking permit; those who don't generally return to find a ticket waiting.

The Wapato Greenway on the opposite side of the island provides access to the Multnomah Channel.

CHAPTER TEN

Exploring Sauvie Island in the Twenty-First Century

The island is flat, which makes it appealing to both bicyclists and casual hikers. A parking area beneath the bridge provides a place to unload bicycles and leave your car.

With no bicycle lanes on the island it can be dangerous when cars travel too fast, so if you're driving you need to be on the lookout for two-wheeled visitors.

Sauvie Island is situated in two counties; Multnomah County holds 2/3 of the land and the rest is in Columbia County. More than 11,000 island acres are designated for exclusive farm use; the other 13,000 acres are owned by the State of Oregon.

Most of that public land is found within the Sauvie Island Wildlife Area.

GETTING THE MOST FROM YOUR ISLAND VISIT

Whether traveling by bicycle, car or boat, Sauvie Island is a great place to get in touch with nature. The roads and trails are flat, the landscape changes with the seasons, and in the spring you can watch the turbulent waters from the dike's protective rim.

Little has changed on Sauvie Island in the past thirty years; being out on the island still provides a walk thru natural lands where wild creatures make their homes.

Sauvie Island; A Step Back in Time

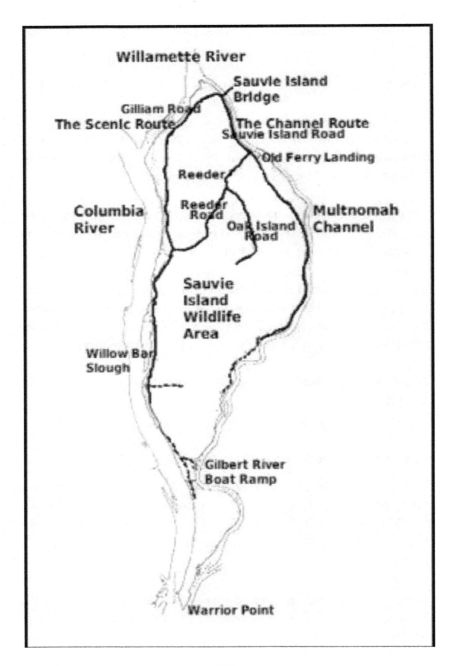

To make your visit more enjoyable take along a couple of waterfowl, bird, tree, plant, wildflower or butterfly identification books. You'll find lots to identify no matter which you take.

If you intend to spend time along the Columbia River beaches bring a chart showing the flags of all countries and one on ship stack markings. Together, they will help you to figure out what each ship might be carrying and its home port.

Sharing island roads with bicyclists requires slower speeds for everyone's safety, and only adds a minute to the time it takes to cross the island.

It will also make life more pleasant for those who live on the island year round. Garbage facilities are limited, so plan on taking your garbage with you when you leave.

This is a special place, one that has thrilled visitors for centuries. With a little extra care from today's visitors, thirty years from now a trip to Sauvie Island will still feel like a step back in time.

EXPLORING THE ISLAND

Unless you arrive by boat, every visit to the island begins at the Sauvie Island Bridge. You'll find it four miles past the St. John's Bridge, along U.S. Highway 30.

On a clear day you can see three snow-capped mountains as you cross the bridge. From left to right they are Mount St. Helens, Mt. Adams and Mt. Hood. St. Helens will be large and has a flattened top, Adams is short, and Hood is large and pointed. The Tualatin Mountain and the old Indian trail are behind you.

Mighty oaks, ash, cottonwood and willows once grew in abundance all over this island, where blue skies, green hills and mountain silhouettes fill the view in every direction. Quiet, yet mighty rivers surround this peaceful land where cattle, sheep and horses graze, and migrating waterfowl calls out overhead.

Flat paved roads travel along the island shores now, forming a horseshoe, with a connecting road going off to the left 2.5 miles down the channel. Gravel roads and hiking trails provide easy access to the island's wildlife areas.

As you leave the bridge you can follow the loop to its end for a scenic drive along the Columbia River, or take the Sauvie Island Road exit off the bridge loop to travel along the Multnomah Channel. Reeder Road connects these two roads, allowing visitors to see it all without too much backtracking.

GILLIAM ROAD - THE SCENIC ROUTE (14.5 miles)

If you follow the bridge loop you will land on Gilliam Road and be heading toward the Willamette and Columbia Rivers. If the skies are clear the views will be awesome with Mount St. Helens and Mt. Hood towering behind the island; Mt. Adams is often visible between them.

You'll find u-pick farms and nurseries scattered all along this road. Many offer fresh produce and plants as well as u-pick opportunities. **Bella Organic & U-pick** is 1.7 miles from the bridge, the **Pumpkin Patch & Corn Maze** 2.1 miles, and **Columbia Farms U-pick** 4.7 miles.

Bella Organic is open from May 31st thru the first week in November between 9am and 6pm. **Bella's Country Kitchen** and a **Beer Garden**, plus wine tasting make it a delightful place to stop. They offer lots of u-pick crops, run a corn maze at Halloween, and put on live music events as well.

U-pick crops on the island begin with strawberries and raspberries in early June; the marionberries ripen in July. U-cut flowers are available mid-July thru October, peaches and nectarines are ready in August, and tomatoes in September. The season ends with pumpkins.

The Pumpkin Patch is open June thru October, from 9am to 6pm, and includes an animal barn where children can see chickens, rabbits, ducks, peacocks, sheep, goats, llama, cows and pigs. They also serve hamburgers and deserts in their **Patio Café**.

Every Labor Day weekend the Pumpkin Patch holds a big Harvest Festival that includes free hayrides, craft making opportunities and a giant hay maze. Music, food and demonstrations are also scheduled. Halloween is big here too.

At Columbia Farms you can pick berries, peppers, tomatoes, flowers, and pumpkins too. They are open Tuesday thru Sunday during the summer and Friday thru Sunday in the fall, between 9am and 5pm.

Here, along the Columbia River shores, two large Indian villages once thrived. The constantly changing shoreline, farming and construction of the dike have completely obliterated their locations.

Watch for brightly painted smokestacks above the dike as you travel; you can see commercial ships on their way to the Willamette River entrance from here.

During high water entire ships come into view; they look like they are floating across fields, barely missing silos and outbuildings, against a backdrop of grain elevators marking the distant shore.

Continuing to travel along Gilliam Road you'll be treated to beautiful river views and plenty of bird watching opportunities.

As you near the 4 mile point, just beyond the nursery with the old trucks planted full of flowers, you'll begin to see large nests sitting on top of platform poles. These are Osprey nests; the birds usually return early in April.

After 6.2 miles you'll come to a stop sign and **Reeder Road**. Turn left and this road will take you back towards the Multnomah Channel. Turn right here to continue along the Columbia River.

Turning right on Reeder Road you'll cross over **The Big Dike** and enter the land of the Multnomahs. It is estimated that more than 800 natives once made their home along this shore.

Although the old Indian village sites have been covered by sand after decades of river dredging, according to the journals of Lewis and Clark these villagers were the ones who came downriver to trade with them near Willow Bar.

You can drive an additional 8.3 miles along the Columbia River, ending at a parking lot where you'll find trails leading to Warrior Point. As you drive you'll be rewarded with gorgeous river views.

Refreshments are available at the **Reeder Beach Store** 1.4 miles to the right; the **Dairy Island Cove Café** is 1.5 miles further up the road, and the **Island Cove Market & Cafe** a mile beyond Dairy Island Cove.

The trees along here are primarily black cottonwood and Oregon ash, but you'll also see alder, willow, cherry, hawthorn and big leaf maple. You'll cross the Columbia County Line about .3 mile past the **Blue Heron Herbary**.

The hiking is easy on any of the wildlife area access roads; you'll find one 2.9 miles north of the stop sign that will take you to Sturgeon Lake and another 1.5 miles further up the road at the **East Side Creek Station**. No motorized vehicles are allowed on these roads but they're flat enough to push a sturdy stroller.

Willow Bar Slough is located across from the Island Cove Market. This little waterway was created when three tiny islands, Pete's, Griffith and Clanaquah, became silted together with the main island to form a sheltered cove.

When this book was first written this cove was home to a live-aboard boating community that I called home; today it is vacant and has been dredged for public access.

It is somewhere along here that Lt. Broughton and Lewis and Clark both made their camps. The noise of the migrating waterfowl that disturbed the sleep of those 1805 visitors can be just as loud today.

Since the road runs along the top of the dike here, you get a gorgeous view across the Columbia River.

As you cross **Rentenaar Road,** look toward the river and you'll see more Osprey platform nests. The one pictured on the next page is shared with a river marker and buoy light.

Rentenaar Road is on your left and leads to a tangle of waterways at the northern end of Sturgeon Lake. It will take you to Big McNary and Little McNary Lakes, Pete's Slough and Sturgeon Lake.

The road turns to gravel 6.1 miles beyond the stop sign, but you can follow it along the Columbia River for an additional 2.2 miles. This is where you'll find the island's best beaches.

All along this portion of the island river beaches are open to the public. Parking areas are found opposite stairways that lead you over the dike to the Columbia.

To park your car here you'll need a Wildlife Area parking permit. Boaters arriving by water can simply drop anchor and boat or swim to shore.

This end of the island offers plenty of secluded beach areas where families can spend the day with the kids, away from the party crowds and wide-open beaches where groups gather.

Collins Beach, the island's only clothing optional beach, begins about a quarter mile beyond the pavement's end.

The **Gilbert River Boat Ramp** is on the left, about a mile beyond the start of the gravel portion of this road. The island is extremely narrow at this point, only about a quarter mile wide, and the boat ramp road is where you can cross to the Multnomah Channel side.

This is the ideal place for a canoeist who wants to get to **Sturgeon Lake** and other wetland areas. The boat ramp is open year round, but access to the Gilbert River and Sturgeon Lake is not allowed from October 31 to April 15 due to hunting.

Drive another 1.3 miles past the boat ramp to where Reeder Road ends and you'll find a large parking area, outhouse and trails leading to the old **lighthouse site** as well as **Warrior Point** on the downriver tip of the island.

Take the trail on the left and you can walk around the edge of **Cunningham Lake** to the Multnomah Channel; it doesn't take long to get there.

If you follow the trail along the Columbia River it will take you past lakes and wetlands all the way to Warrior Point. The **Namuit Indian Village** once occupied these beaches, and this was where the tribe planted their burial canoes.

Warrior Point was also the temporary site of Nathaniel Wyeth's island business and the location of a successful wooden ship building industry in the early 1900's.

The rocks just offshore have always been a danger to watercraft; they rise and fall from view with the tide. From here the city of St. Helens can be seen across the channel.

When you make your return drive, it is 8.3 miles back to the stop sign where Gilliam and Reeder Road meet. If you take the Reeder Road connection, the drive back to the bridge is 2 miles shorter and you'll see fresh scenery.

REEDER ROAD – THE CONNECTION (4.3 miles)

This road crosses the island, connecting the road running along the Columbia to one that runs along the Multnomah Channel. The parking area on the right, 1.1 miles inland, has a handicap accessible trail that leads toward the center of the island, as well as toilets and an informational kiosk.

This is a good place for waterfowl watching; in the late fall the skies will suddenly fill with birds as they are flushed from the nearby wetlands.

Continue driving along Reeder Road another 2 miles and turn right on **NW Oak Island Road**. This is the Oak Island Detour; it will take you to the center of the island.

Oak Island Road Detour

The **Gilbert River** curves along this road's west edge and fields stretch out to the east. Once a dairyman's island, this is the location of the last dairy.

The part of the island is made up of natural gravel and heavy rock; this rocky base is part of the original island core. Giant oak trees once grew along the entire length of Sauvie Island; the oak ridge seen here is all that remains and includes trees that began growing before Columbus discovered America.

The paved road turns to gravel after 6.2 miles. A gate is located where the gravel begins, blocking access to the area from October thru mid April; the balance of the year the gate is open for everyone between 4am and 10pm.

Follow this gravel road one mile to the **Oak Island Trail**; it's a maintained pathway with no inclines. This 2.5 mile loop circles a peninsula that juts out into Sturgeon Lake and also provides access to **Steelman Lake**. It takes about an hour to walk the entire loop.

Three **prehistoric village sites** were discovered along this route; seasonal water changes have washed away their remains. When the vegetation is sparse you can still see the imprint left by the old **dance rings**; they appear as circular indentations in the ground.

Sauvie Island; A Step Back in Time

Back on Reeder Road

Back at Reeder Road, continue toward the channel and you'll soon see the 1980 schoolhouse where the **Sauvie Island Academy** now operates.

Charlton Road, on the left just past the school, leads to the **Sauvie Island Grange**. A stop sign .2 mile beyond this point means you are near the Multnomah Channel.

If you turn left you'll be heading back towards the bridge; go to the right on Sauvie Island Road and you'll find more historic and natural areas to visit.

SAUVIE ISLAND ROAD - THE CHANNEL ROUTE (9.2 miles total)

If you're arriving at Sauvie Island Road by way of Reeder Road, you can turn left and go 2.5 miles back to the bridge if you're ready to leave the island.

Otherwise, turn right and take the 6.7 mile paved road that travels along the Multnomah Channel towards Warrior Point.

The **Multnomah Channel** is only 7 miles long; for smaller boats it's a calmer route between the Willamette and Columbia Rivers.

The channel water and riverside vegetation provide habitat for waterfowl, heron, cormorants and kingfishers. Boat docks and moorages dot both sides of this waterway. The Multnomah Channel is part of the Willamette River Greenway.

From the Bridge to Reeder Road (2.5 miles)

If you're taking the Sauvie Island Road exit off the bridge loop you can stock up on snacks at the **Cracker Barrel Store** located at the base of the bridge, before heading out. They also sell SIWA parking passes, which are a necessity for anyone planning to leave their car to explore the island on foot.

Leaving the bridge on Sauvie Island Road, after about a mile you will come to the **Howell Territorial Park** and the Greek revival-styled **Bybee-Howell House**.

Located on the east side of the road, the park covers 93 acres and includes a home built in 1856. Managed by Metro Parks and Greenspaces, the park is open to the public from sunrise to sunset and part of the **Willamette River Greenway**.

The trail north of the old house leads to **Howell Lake**, an open-water wetland. This trail is popular with bird watchers. The house is currently not open to the public.

The old orchard contains a number of rare heirloom apple trees, and the rose garden is filled with heirloom roses. The Heron sculpture was created by Portland artist Tom Hardy.

Back on Sauvie Island Road, about a mile beyond the park, **Kruger's U-pick** offers fresh vegetables, a picnic area, children's activities and a corn maze. They also rent out space for weddings and special events.

The farm's **Island Grill** and u-cut flowers entice visitors to sit for a while. Along the road colorful fields filled with flowers and nursery stock present a pleasing view.

Sauvie Island; A Step Back in Time

This is some of the island's highest land. Reeder Road is located 2.5 miles beyond the bridge. If you turn right, it will take you across the island to the Columbia River along the Reeder Road connection.

All the Way to the End (6.7 miles)

Continue travelling along Sauvie Island Road and after about a quarter mile you'll arrive at the **Sauvie Island Visitor Center**; it's on the right. The staff there can answer any questions you have about public access to the wildlife area.

Across the road from the visitors center is the entrance to **Wapato Greenway**. You'll find a paved boat launch here; the ramp and park are open from 7am to 7pm, providing channel access, picnic tables and vault toilets. The boat ramp is located near the old **Burlington Ferry Landing**.

The Greenway's **Wapato State Park** is managed by the Oregon State Parks Department. It's part of the **Virginia Lakes Area**, a significant natural and wetland area, and includes a transient boat dock known as **Hadley's Landing**. This park provides public access to the 280-acre Virginia Lakes Area.

Continuing along the channel on Sauvie Island Road you'll travel past the **Sauvie Island Farms** u-pick fields and the sweet smelling **Lavender Farm**.

Sauvie Island Farms offers strawberries, raspberries, blueberries, marionberries, peaches, pears, nectarines, corn, tomatoes, peppers, melons and u-cut flowers. Open 8am to 7pm Monday thru Saturday between June and September, special Halloween and pumpkin-related activities are also held here every October.

The Lavender Farm has a garden that contains more than 1800 lavender plants. You can cut your own fresh lavender here, walk the paths of the Victorian garden, or visit the little shop where you'll find lavender scented gifts and fresh plants. Classes in wreath and lavender crafts are taught here. The farm is open May thru October, Tuesday thru Sunday, from 10am to 5pm.

Making your way along Sauvie Island Road, at 4.4 miles you'll see a sign pointing toward the location of Nathaniel Wyeth's island city of **Fort William**. There is nothing to see, just a sign. The town was situated near the water, like the Indian villages that were built there before it. This is also where the first ferry landing was located.

Rocky Point Marina is two miles further up the road and the Columbia County line is just beyond that. The road turns to gravel .4 mile beyond this point; just before that you'll see the old pump house and tower where they can control the island's water level.

This is the entrance to the SIWA **West Side Checking Station**. Open only to licensed hunters during hunting season, fishermen and hikers will find many great sites along this section's trails the balance of the year. When you are tired of exploring the trails you can return to the bridge.

If you have not yet toured the Columbia side of the island take Reeder Road east to where it joins up with Gilliam Road for more fun.

TOURING THE ISLAND BY BOAT

What better way to see an island than from its surrounding waterway?

Whether you launch your boat at St. Johns, St. Helens, or one of the three boat ramps found along the island's edge, a boat allows you to see the island the way early explorers saw it. Until 1950 travelling by boat was the only way to get on or off the island.

If you want to travel around the entire island it will take you the better part of a day; this is Oregon's largest island. There are nearly 40 miles of shoreline.

A trip around the island makes for a relaxing weekend outing, and you'll find a number of spots where you can drop anchor or tie up. Boat gas is available along the mainland side of the channel only.

Travelling with the current on the Columbia River will save time and gas. Your journey begins in the **Willamette River** where it branches off to the left to form the channel. This end of the island is privately owned and has no public access. Travelling along the Willamette River you will soon spot the protective rise of The Big Dike.

As you enter the **Columbia River** you'll be passing **Belle Vue Point**. The view upriver on a sunny day will show you why Lt. Broughton was so taken with his first glimpse of Mt. Hood from this point.

Along the island shore you'll begin to see sandy beaches, homes perched high above the river where inhabitants have a protected view of the water, and a peaceful farmland setting.

The Columbia River is at times a busy waterway filled with commercial traffic and pleasure craft travelling side by side. After passing Channel Marker #19 you'll see a rocky point that shelters the entrance to **Willow Bar Slough**.

Dredging has turned the three small islands that were once found here into a peninsula, changing its appearance from what it was when visited by Lt. Broughton and the Lewis and Clark Expedition.

The beaches beyond this point are mostly managed by the **Sauvie Island Wildlife Area** and are open to the public from 4am to 10pm seven days a week.

Camping is not allowed on the land but the river offers many delightful places to drop anchor. The island's sandy beaches extend for long distances at low tide; when pulling in near shore make sure to watch your depth as well as the tide.

Stay away from the land when you come around **Warrior Point** on the far end of the island; the submerged rocks here can be dangerous and have caught many boaters off guard. Hit them and you'll cause great damage to your boat.

The mainland town of **St. Helens** is located opposite Warrior Point; it offers a large public dock. From there, a short walk will take you into town for supplies.

Entering the **Multnomah Channel** you will be leaving most of the commercial river traffic behind. Although tugboats still travel the channel, it is no longer the pathway for commercial vessels that it was during the island's early days.

You will soon arrive at the entrance to Sauvie Island's **Gilbert River** and the **Crane Lake Channel**. The depth of these waterways fluctuates with the tide and can get quite shallow; at high tide small boats can follow the river all the way into **Sturgeon Lake**.

Your boat's draft, along with the water conditions, will help you to decide whether or not this side trip is open to you. If you've brought along an inflatable or a small boat it should be easy.

A little further up the Multnomah Channel you'll find **Coon Island**. This tiny tree covered public island has its own boat dock and is open to all on a first-come basis.

Created for boaters, it is inaccessible except by water. There is enough room for 4-5 boats plus a couple of tents; the island has no toilets.

Continuing toward the Willamette River you'll pass lots of houseboats and moorages from this point on. Remember to slow your boat speed to 5 mph as you pass to minimize your wake and possible damage. Fast boats toss these homes and watercraft about wildly, so be thoughtful.

Cruising beneath the Sauvie Island Bridge it's just a short distance to the island's upper point and the Willamette River which signals the completion of your 40-mile boat trip.

APPENDIX

Sauvie Island Plants, Trees and Wildlife

WAPATO

The dark green leaves of the Wapato plant can be seen along the shallow edge of island lakes. The waxy white summer blossoms have bright yellow centers.

In the fall small tubers mature along the roots; they are hard and white inside, sometimes growing up to a foot long. This is what the Indians gathered. The root has a very bitter taste when eaten raw, but the bitterness disappears when boiled or baked.

CAMAS

The Indians once baked the bulbs of the Blue Camas in rock-lined pits. The early summer blossoms are bright blue which makes it easy to distinguish this edible plant from the poisonous Death Camas.

You will find it growing along the island's wetlands, almost as abundantly as when it was one of the primary vegetables for island Indians. The plants reach a height of one to two feet and have one-inch-wide onion-like bulbs that grow just below the soil.

OAK TREES

The oak trees on Sauvie Island silhouette the sky with their huge, outstretched appearance.

Many stand a solitary vigil surrounded by cultivated fields, the last of the open woodland that once covered much of the island.

These might oaks add an artistic touch to the land when autumn takes their leaves through a variety of colors. Some of the larger oak trees have survived centuries of flooding.

WILLOW TREES

Willow trees do very well on the island. The fact that water lies only a short distance beneath the soil makes it a wonderful place for the willow to take root.

They have long, slim, gracefully-pointed leaves hanging in clusters that sometimes touch the ground.

COTTONWOOD TREES

The island's river banks are lined with cottonwood trees, and when the wind ruffles the tapering leaf it exposes a white underside.

The female tree produces lots of small seeds covered with a cotton-like substance which gives the tree its name.

COMMON FOOTPRINTS

The abundance of wet ground on the island provides lots of opportunities to observe the tracks of some of the island's smaller inhabitants.

The lucky visitor will catch a glimpse of one up close.

Here are a few common tracks to get you started.

Illustration - Row one: skunk, opossum, and raccoon. Row two: muskrat, mink, and beaver. Row three: red fox, dog, and black - tailed deer.

GREAT BLUE HERON

Most often seen standing in mud or shallow water, the Great Blue Heron is common on the island year round.

The mature adult has a six foot wingspan, is slate gray in color, and flies with the neck folded back rather than outstretched.

Herons live on a diet of mice, fish, and snakes, and are sometimes seen standing in open fields as they wait for lunch to run past.

SANDHILL CRANE

A migratory bird, the Sandhill Crane passes through every spring and fall.

The crane's body is about four feet long, and they have a wingspan of seven feet.

These birds are gray, with a red forehead and a short bill. The crane flies with its neck and tail extended.

You will see them standing in open fields, looking very tall, with a long extended neck and legs.

RING-NECKED PHEASANT

Residing here year-round, the pheasant is a ground bird that's a little larger than a chicken with a long pointed tail.

The male sports a red eye patch, bright green head and white neck ring. They are often seen running across the road in brush-surrounded areas.

CANADA GOOSE

Every fall huge flocks of Canadian Geese cover island fields and lakes. These birds have long black necks and a white face patch.

Although most are just passing thru, it is not unusual to see them on the island year round. When disturbed they move as a group, with a great deal of noise; their sound and size makes them easy to spot.

ISLAND HAWKS

Hawks are easy to spot too, and fun to watch. When viewed from underneath, they are also very easy to identify once you learn the three common shapes.

Hawks are grouped into three families - Buteos, Accipiters and Falcons; each has a different body and wing style, making them easy to tell apart.

Pictured at the top is the Falcon, lower left Buteo, and lower right Accipiter.

FALCONS have long narrow pointed wings and their own special hunting technique. If you see a bird diving on its prey at full speed, it's probably a falcon. Although rare, you could encounter a Prairie Falcon on the island. They are spectacular fliers and occasionally seen here in the fall.

BUTEOS have broad wings with rounded tips, chunky bodies and broad tails. They like to fly and soar in wide circles as they search open fields for rodents. The most common Sauvie Island Buteo is the Red Tailed Hawk.

RED TAILED HAWK

The Red Tailed Hawk is a large, broad-winged bird of prey that nests on the island; it can be seen year round. It has a wingspan of 45-58 inches, and the female is larger than the male.

The upper part of a Red Tailed Hawk's tail is bright red, making it easy to identify when seen from the right angle.

ACCIPITERS have much shorter wings than the Buteos. Coupled with a slim body and long tail, they are easy to tell apart once you memorize the shapes. Accipiters fly with rapid wing beats and then sail for long periods of time. They perch in secluded places, darting out to pursue prey.

The Coopers Hawk with its reddish-streaked breast belongs to the Accipiter family. Although seldom seen, they nest on bulky platforms built of sticks and twigs high above the ground.

The Sharp-Shinned Hawk is a smaller version of the Coopers Hawk. The males have a wingspan of 20-23 inches and a square tail tip. In the winter you might spot a Goshawk, but they are rare. This bird has a dark head and a wreath of lighter gray feathers just above its eyes.

Appendix Artwork by Cathy Dvorak

All of the pen and ink drawings contained in this appendix appeared in the original edition of this book and were drawn by Cathy Dvorak.

INDEX

A

Academy of Natural Sciences in Philadelphia · 45
Acorn pits · 26
Archeological Investigations Northwest · 26
Arthur Post Office · 80
Astoria Trading Post · 37

B

Ball, John · 40
Bella Organic & U-pick · 96
Belle Vue Point · 33, 34, 112
Big Dike · 71, 72, 75, 84, 99, 112
Big and Little McNary Lakes · 102
Blue Heron Herbary · 101
British Northwest Company · 37
Broughton, Lt. William · 32, 33, 35, 79, 101, 112
Burlington Ferry · 74, 81, 110
Bybee, James · 54, 56
Bybee-Howell House · 56, 108

C

Call's River · 32, 79
Canoe burial · 23, 24, 46
Carved images · 28, 29
Charlton, Joseph · 54
Chief Cassino · 22, 25
Chinook tribe · 16
Cline, James · 52
Collins Beach · 103
Columbia County · 78, 111
Columbia Farms · 97, 98
Columbia River · 23, 31, 32, 37, 39, 40, 41, 43, 44, 53, 65, 69, 79, 80, 85, 90, 91, 93, 95, 96, 98, 99, 100, 101, 103, 105, 107, 109, 111, 112
Columbia River Fishing & Trading Company · 39
Confederated Tribe · 27
Coon Island · 114
Cooper, William · 52
Courtney, Walker · 42, 43
Cracker Barrel Store · 108
Crane Lake · 76
Crane Lake Channel · 113
Cunningham Lake · 105

D

Dairy Creek · 85, 86
Dairy Island Cove Cafe · 100
Donation Land Law · 50, 61

E

East Side Creek Station · 101

F

Federal Flood Control Act · 70
Ferry · 63, 74, 81, 84, 85, 86, 87, 111

First Oregon Events
    1st criminal trial · 16, 43, 45
    1st farmers - 40
    1st fish processing factory · 39
    1st island American baby · 52
    1st plaster house · 54
    1st religious funeral · 44
    1st Oregon school · 44
    1st school teacher · 40
    1st sermon west of Rockies · 44
    1st white couple married · 44
    1st white men on the island · 33
    1st white woman to die · 44
    1st white woman to travel the Oregon Trail · 51
Flathead Indians · 19, 43
Fort Hall · 41
Fort Vancouver · 37, 39, 40, 41, 46, 47
Fort William · 16, 42, 43, 45, 46, 47, 110
Franchere, Gabriel · 37
Francis-Alice · 79
Fraser River Culture · 15
Fur Traders · 3, 16, 31

G

Gilbert River · 71, 90, 103, 106, 113
Gilbert River Boat Ramp · 103
Gillihan, Martin · 52
Gray, Capt. Robert · 31

H

H.M.S. Chatham · 32
Hadley's Landing · 110
Howell, Benjamin · 54, 56
Howell, Joseph · 56
Howell Lake · 56, 108
Howell Territorial Park · 56, 108
Hubbard, Thomas J. · 16, 43
Hudson Bay Company · 11, 37, 39, 40, 42, 46, 47, 48, 51
Hutchinson Ranch · 74

I

Island Cove Market & Cafe · 100
Island Grill · 108
Island Wapato · 84

J

Jewett, Leonard · 52

K

Kruger's U-pick · 108

L

Lambert, Captain · 41
Lavender Farm · 110
Lee, Daniel · 44
Lee, Jason · 44
Lewis & Clark · 11, 21, 24, 35, 79, 100, 101, 112
Lighthouse · 77, 78, 83, 104
Linnton · 50, 82
Little Sturgeon Lake - 71Logie Trail · 52
Logie, James and Isabelle · 47, 48, 51, 52
Lot Whitcomb · 79

Lucea Mason · 79

M

Marquam Lake · 47, 71
May Dacre · 41, 42
McCormick, Charles · 81
McCormick, Hamlin - 81
McIntire, Horace · 54
McLoughlin, John · 25, 37, 46, 47
McQuinn, Alexander · 52
Menzies, James · 54
Miller Family · 54
Millionaire Lake - 76
Milwaukie · 50
Mission Society of the Episcopal Church · 16, 43
Missionaries · 17, 43, 44, 46, 47
Moar, Jonathan · 52
Morgan Family · 53
Mount St. Helens · 9, 95, 96
Mouse Lake · 71
Mouth of the Willamette Post Office · 80
Mt. Adams · 9, 95, 96
Mt. Hood · 9, 34, 95, 96, 112
Mud Lake - 76
Multnomah Channel · 32, 41, 79, 96, 99, 103, 105, 107, 113, 114
Multnomah County · 54, 56, 93
Multnomah Indians · 11, 15, 16, 19, 22, 35, 38, 99
Multnomah Island · 3, 12, 13, 31

N

National Historic Landmark · 26
Nuttall, Thomas · 45

O

Oak Island · 4, 106
Oregon City · 50
Oregon Department of Fish and Wildlife · 11, 89
Oregon Historical Society · 2, 6, 15, 29
Oregon Territory · 3, 49, 50, 51, 56
Oregon Trail · 5, 17, 41, 49, 51
Oregon Wildlife Commission · 89

P

Pete's Slough · 102
Pittman, Anna Maria · 44
Population · 14, 20, 24, 37, 82, 83, 88
Portland · 5, 9, 10, 50, 62, 79, 81, 86, 87, 88, 108
Pumpkin Patch · 97, 98

R

Racetrack Lake - 76
Reeder Beach Store · 100
Reeder Point · 37
Reeder, Simon · 52, 53
Rentenaar · 101, 102
Roberts, George · 24
Rocky Point Marina · 111

S

Sauvé, Laurent · 11, 47
Sauvie Island Farms · 110

Sauvie Island Grange · 80, 107
Sauvie Island Visitor Center · 109
Sauvie Island Wildlife Management Area · 3, 11, 89, 91, 93, 113
Scappoose · 10
Shepard, Cyrus · 44
Shipbuilding industry · 17, 105
St. Helens · 77, 78, 79, 81, 82, 105, 111, 113
St. Johns · 111
Star of Oregon · 17
Steelman Lake · 106
Stone carvings · 15, 29
Sturgeon Lake · 37, 77, 90, 101, 102, 103, 106, 113
Sunken Village Dig · 26

T

Taylor, James · 47, 48, 52, 80
The Manzanita · 77
Thompson, David · 37
Thornburgh · 16, 43, 45
Tibbits, Calvin · 40
Townsend, J.K. · 45, 46
Tualatin Valley · 41, 52

U

U.S. Coast Guard · 77
United States Exploring Expedition · 12
University of Oregon · 27, 56
U-pick crops · 6, 13, 96, 97, 110

V

Vancouver, Capt. George · 31, 32
Virginia Lakes Area · 110

W

Wakanasese Island · 3, 11, 13, 19
Walker, Ellis · 54
Wapama · 82
Wapato plant · 11, 20, 21, 22, 36, 123
Wapato Greenway · 109
Wapato Inlet · 79
Wapato Island · 11, 13
Wapato State Park · 110
Warrior Branch · 79
Warrior Point · 77, 100, 104, 105, 107, 113
Warrior Rock · 32, 41, 67, 77
Washougal · 36
West Side Checking Station · 111
White, Matthew · 52
Willamette Falls · 50
Willamette River · 17, 33, 34, 36, 50, 65, 79, 85, 88, 96, 98, 107, 112, 114
Willamette River Greenway · 108
Willamette Valley · 17
Wilkes, Commodore Charles · 12, 79
Willow Bar · 69, 100, 101
Willow Bar Slough · 112
Wyeth Island · 3, 11, 13, 16, 39, 110
Wyeth, Nathanial · 3, 11, 16, 17, 39, 40, 41, 42, 43, 44, 45, 46, 49, 50, 51, 52, 105, 110

Y

Young America · 79
Young, Ewing · 46, 47

ABOUT THE AUTHOR

KiKi Canniff began her love affair with Sauvie Island as a child during the 1950's. Two decades later she moved to the island where she spent her idle hours hiking, canoeing and exploring its public lands and historic places.

After writing *Sauvie Island; A Step Back in Time*, KiKi spent the next twenty years writing a series of Pacific Northwest guidebooks.

Now a retired tax consultant, she also writes books for individuals and small business owners looking for ways to pay less tax. For more information on KiKi's books visit www.OneMorePress.com.

Please Post a Review on Amazon

If you enjoyed this book, and purchased it from Amazon, I hope you will take a moment to post a positive review. Click here to REVIEW THIS BOOK.

Once you get to the book page, simply click on the link for all customer reviews; this will give you a button to click to create your own review.

Thanks!
KiKi

OTHER BOOKS BY KIKI CANNIFF

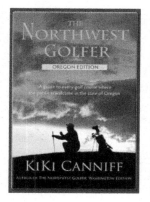

THE NORTHWEST GOLFER provides Oregon and Washington golfers with a quick and easy way to locate every golf course in the Pacific Northwest where the public is welcome.

Golfers in Oregon and Washington can play on courses designed by famous architects, tee off in the shadow of gorgeous snow-capped mountains, and hone their skills on some pretty unique terrain.

The Northwest Golfer provides golfers with an easy way to keep the region's more than 350 public golf courses at their fingertips. There is one volume for Oregon golfers, and another one for those in Washington.

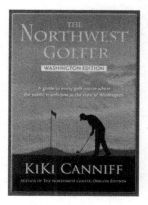

Both books are laid out in an identical format, with each state divided into four vertical sections. Cities and courses are then listed alphabetically.

Each listing begins with a handy reference line that reveals the course's yardage, par, number of holes, and price range. This is followed by contact information, along with details about the course terrain, designer, history, facilities available, green fees, equipment rental rates, discount times and more.

Golfers in Oregon or Washington have enjoyed *The Northwest Golfer* for decades; it was first published in 1986.

www.OneMorePress.com

Made in the USA
Las Vegas, NV
27 February 2021